ᴀlife worth
RIDING

IW

Advance Praise

'Out of adversity comes knowledge, overcoming depression gives hope, overcoming our own loss of self-worth gives us empathy for others, learning we are not alone in our quest for the meaning of our lives connects us to ourselves, to God, our families, others around us and the whole human race.

From time to time, you may ask: 'Why am I here? I am so lost. What do I have to offer anyone? I don't know what to do. How will I ever get out of this?' Sandi Simons has had to face all of these questions, and has learned how to change her thinking and her life, coming through in such a way she can help others. When you read her story you will be inspired. You too can make it through the hard times in your life. No situation is not changeable, fixable, or lasts forever; good can and will come out of any situation when you see it through. Life is changing, will change, can change, and will carry us through to a better day and give us hope. When all the advice around you seems to get you down *A Life Worth Riding* will give you courage to be yourself and know what's right for you and you alone.'

— John Lyons, natural horsemanship trainer, recipient of Equitana USA's Modern Masters Award for Outstanding Horsemanship and the University of Louisville's John W Galbreath Award for outstanding contributions to the horse industry.

A life worth RIDING

SANDI SIMONS
WITH FELICITY WISCHER

FINCH PUBLISHING
SYDNEY

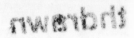

A Life Worth Riding

First published in 2013 in Australia and New Zealand by Finch Publishing Pty Limited, ABN 49 057 285 248, Suite 2207, 4 Daydream Street, Warriewood, NSW, 2102, Australia.

13 87654321

There is a National Library of Australia Cataloguing-in-Publication entry available at the National Library.

Edited by Karen Gee
Editorial assistance by Tricia Corteze
Text typeset in Adobe Garamond Pro by Meg Dunworth
Cover design by Designerbility
Back cover photograph by Stacie Robinson
All internal photos suppplied by Sandi Simons, unless stated otherwise.
Printed by Griffin Press

Finch titles can be viewed and purchased at **www.finch.com.au**

Contents

For David, my rock, my mentor, my beacon in the darkest of nights, my soul mate and my love. Thank you for always believing in me and supporting me no matter what. Without you there would be no story to tell. We have created the true meaning of forever ...

Introduction

Through the work I do with women and horses I have often been asked how I came to do what I do. Some of the wonderful women I have had the privilege of meeting and working with have wanted to know more about my life story and what motivated me to start the Confidence Clinics and Camps for women and their horses. I can only assume it is because they think we share some common bond in who we are and why we ride. Perhaps it is because they have heard me reflect on some of my own riding and life experiences as I listened to them when they came to a clinic or camp.

Initially I found it a little daunting that anyone would be interested enough in my story to pick up a book and read about it, warts and all. I asked myself and those closest to me 'Would you be interested in reading my autobiography?' And the very fact that it is now in existence means the answer was obviously yes. Once I looked at it from this perspective I began to reflect upon the project from a different point of view. Who would read it? Is it that important? What can writing about my life achieve? Would it uncover anything that would be of benefit to anyone? What can it give to someone? Would it be of interest to someone? Do I want to revisit my past?

I concluded that telling my story would perhaps help other women, like-minded, kindred spirits, to realise I truly did understand much of what they were experiencing and feeling. Everyone's story is unique and there is no doubt in my mind that sharing and listening (something which we women are very good at) can be a mutually beneficial experience for those who care to take the time to do so. We all need to be heard, we all need to be understood, we all need sometimes to feel inspiration from within and from others, and we often need to find clarity and insight into the many questions and challenges we face while travelling through life.

Writing this book has been a wonderfully cathartic experience. It has taught me a lot about who I am and where I have come from, and has reconfirmed who I am today. Some of the memories from my upbringing have made me feel great sadness and I have had some anxious moments reliving my past; however, I wanted my recollections to be 'real' and not an exaggerated version of the past. Nor was the past to be glossed over or watered down. This is not a finger-pointing exercise, there are no accusations, there is no blame laid at anyone's feet. This is completely about me – quite simply, this is my story.

I hope you enjoy reading this and that in some small way you can benefit from my journey and experiences.

Chapter 1

A taste of things to come

I am me. I am who I am meant to be. I am my past, my present and who I want to be. I am not anyone, I am all three. I am a work in progress. I am a destiny. I am who I choose to be. I am me. – Author unknown

It was a day just like any other day. In fact there was nothing very particular about this day. It was neither sunny nor cold, dull nor raining – just a day, just like any other.

I watched as the women gathered around each other tentatively handing out milk, sugar and mugs. Most of them were strangers to one another but they were brought together by their horses at one of my Confidence Clinics. I sat back and wondered about what the weekend would reveal. I learn something new at every clinic – we all have something to offer, even if we don't think we do. Each clinic starts out with the participants sitting in a circle and having a chat over a cuppa. 'Why are you here?' I ask them. For some reason I always turn and ask this question to the person sitting immediately to my left. That day was no different and so the women started to talk one by one about themselves and their journey with their horses. Little did I know what was about to unfold. It would affect me so profoundly, not just on that day but for many, many days to come.

She was a slim woman, somewhere in her twenties I would guess, with brown hair, dark eyes and dressed in dark browns; arms crossed defensively over her body protecting her from anything getting in. She had a strange mix of superiority and indifference combined with a vulnerability, desolation and apathy that oozed from her very being. But it was her eyes that said it all. I looked into them and my stomach lurched. I felt myself reeling backwards with a whole cavalcade of emotions. I knew that look. I had seen it before, many years ago, staring back at me in the mirror when I was at the lowest ebb in my life. When you see what is looking back at you, really see it, it is as if a stranger is staring at you, someone who is lurking there, someone you have never known or acknowledged who lives within you – it is a frightening and overwhelming experience. It is then and only then that you realise how far you have fallen and how alone and isolated you have become.

It was her turn to speak and even though everyone was quiet and respectful the young woman started to sob and sob, gut-wrenching sobs that seemed to come from the very bottom of her soul. Later she sent me a letter which revealed how close she had been to taking her own life.

Dear Sandi,

I can quite literally say that you have saved my life. I had planned how I was going to terminate the pain and depression, snuff out the anger, isolation and confusion – there was only one day left until I was getting in my car and driving head-on into the traffic to end it all.

So what was I going to do the day before? I had nothing planned – why would I? I came along with my friend to your clinic. My friend had no idea I was thinking of ending my life and her insistence that I go came through her seeing the struggles I was having in my horse training, nothing else. Full of negativity and anger I deliberately thought about how I, Miss Superior Dressage Rider, would go along and sit on the sidelines, waiting to find the flaws in the teaching and training methods of this Sandi Simons woman. Of course, I knew it all. My ego was enormous!

This was no ordinary clinic; I was gobsmacked. I had never been to a clinic where the day started with everyone sitting in a circle and sharing parts of themselves and the reasons that brought us all to be there at the same time, looking for answers. I remember you turning to the lady on your left and asking her 'Why are you here?' You asked each one of us that question and one by one we all started talking. I was sitting immediately to your right and so I was going to be the last person to speak. I rehearsed what I was going to say in my head as each one spoke. Basically, my internal dialogue went like this: 'I am a pretty shit-hot rider, I have ridden at a level that all you other idiots could only dream about, I have been around horses all my life, I don't have a confidence issue with riding because I am so good, I teach people myself and know all there is to know about riding dressage ... despite the fact that I am falling apart inside after a long and disastrous relationship and I've only ever had one 'good horse' that I have been trying to replace for years. I've been through a series of others that do not quite measure up and my current horse keeps as far away from me as possible. I'll just get another one. I have a tough and rewarding job that I am damned good at, I've have had a happy and stable upbringing with a wonderful father and mother and brother. There's nothing wrong with me ... oh, by the way, did I mention that tomorrow I am committing suicide?!'

You know now that I didn't say any of this of course, but I felt you watching me as I sat half listening to what was being said around that circle; it was just the tape playing in my head but about halfway through all of the various stories something miraculous happened. There was a shift; no, more like an earthquake threatening to explode in my brain. All of a sudden I was in a room with a bunch of total strangers and I had never felt more comfortable in all my life. I realised that these people truly cared for each other, regardless of their achievements and how wonderful (or not) they thought they were. Everyone was embraced, loved and accepted. There was not one ounce of criticism expressed. All this was facilitated by you, Sandi, who listened to every one of us as we spoke, like we were the most important person in the world. You really listened. Finally I had found my soft place to fall – there was nothing but encouragement for one another and a true sense of kindred spirits being brought together; wonderful, strong, empowering women. There was a sort of unsaid bond as we sat side by side with each other sharing our stories, each listening, really listening to one another. When it came my turn to speak I felt this enormous burst of heaving sobs come from deep down within me. I couldn't stop crying and you looked straight at me and instantly knew the truth. I didn't have to say a word. That day I was given a true understanding of the power of womanhood and that it was okay to be comfortable with who I am and how I was feeling. I am as I am and all of us are a work in progress. At any given time, we do not necessarily have all the answers for where we are at and why we are there – and that's perfectly all right, perfectly acceptable!

Sandi, you have enabled me to open my eyes and realise that just because I was where I was or had lost confidence in myself my life was not the failure that I had so doggedly perceived it to be, it was in fact my greatest gift to myself because it allowed me to embrace all that I was, had been and were about to become as a woman and as a person.

I received that letter nearly three years ago and this young woman is now working her way forward and onwards with her life. It hasn't been easy and she has made some mistakes but that's okay because at least she has a life now. She has goals, and I see her try to seize the opportunities around her. She talks about the future rather than dwelling in the past. She treats herself with kindness (most of the time) and has learnt to be patient with herself. And although the journey over the past few years has sometimes been a slow and rocky one at least she is here, alive, to be experiencing it. They say that things happen for a reason and who would have known that coming to one of my clinics one day, out of the blue because she had nothing better to do, full of cynicism and anger, would have saved her life?

I count my blessings that for whatever reason this beautiful young woman came to my clinic – whatever it is in the universe that brings strangers together at pivotal points in their lives – it was on this day, this seemingly ordinary day several years ago, that we met.

Life is a culmination of many twists and turns that bring us to where we are at this very moment. Throughout the stories of others, and our own story, we will find many wonderful, often challenging and sometimes just plain nasty, destructive people who have shaped our lives and helped us become the women we are today and in the future, whatever that may hold.

I hope you find inspiration from the many colourful characters you may have had the privilege of knowing along this road that is your life, just as I have. Perhaps you will be able to relate to some of my story.

Chapter 2

In the beginning

My story began on 23 October 1963 in Heathcote, a small rural town in northern Victoria. My dad was always a bit of a joker and when I asked him, as all children do at some point in their early life, where I came from, he told me he went to the drive-in with Mum one day and somehow or other they came home with me! My arrival saw me join my four older siblings. I was, and still am as you may have gathered, the baby of the family and the second girl. The eldest children in my family were twins and they were very close – a girl and a boy; two years later along came another boy and then two years after him was another boy, until fifteen months later I popped along.

Heathcote was a typical Australian country town back when I was growing up; everybody knew everyone else and life was simple. I had a rather idyllic early childhood.

As a little girl I was closest to my brother who was just fifteen months older than I. He never wanted to go to school and leave me according to Mum and would hide down the street at the local post office so he could sneak back home to be with me. We were very, very close but I was too young to remember much of his adoration in those early years. I think we were so close because of our closeness in age.

My next brother was a bad asthmatic and was always sick. His fragile health meant he got a lot of attention from everyone. When I was two years old we moved from Heathcote to Rochester because of his asthma, but this also enabled my father, a mechanic, to find work.

My father worked for the local shire and my mother was a cook who worked at the local hotel and then later at the local hospital. My mother made sure our home was run like a well-oiled machine. My friends would come over after school and raid our fridge or freezer because Mum always had delicious homemade cakes, slices and fudges. For those first few years in Rochester, family life seemed fairly normal.

I was a tomboy from the very beginning, largely because I was the youngest and had to keep up with my three big brothers. My childhood was spent doing all the usual things that country kids in particular do: we rode pushbikes, motorbikes and horses (not all at once!) and played a lot of sport. When the heat of summer came to Rochester we spent a lot of time swimming in the Campaspe River. Life was busy and fun.

Life, however, has a way of taking many twists and turns – sometimes they are not for the better. When I was in grade one my childhood innocence was taken away from me in the cruellest and most destructive way imaginable. One day I was late for the bus from school and as a result I ended up at a neighbour's place. Their teenage son was at home and it was on that day he sexually abused me. Tragically, I know now that this is not uncommon and I have met many who have suffered the same ordeal. There are so many women in the world who have been abused, some so horrifically that it is almost unimaginable that one human being can inflict such pain and horror on another. Back then I didn't understand what had happened. I was only five years old and not much more than a baby. A little dark cloud formed in my mind from this moment of intense emotional and physical pain. It wasn't until I was much older that I realised what sexual abuse was and understood what had happened to me was very, very wrong. Nobody knew what had happened. It was my burden to carry on my own.

For many years after if I heard anyone talk about anything related to sex I would inwardly cringe. I thought about that horrible incident for years. In my mind, I felt like I had done something wrong but I didn't really know what. This confused me and my turmoil was relentless, becoming overwhelming at times. This incident was to play a really damaging part in my life. I felt isolated and alone, feelings that were going to become a repetitive theme in my life for a long while. The scars that were left mentally and subsequently how I behaved when I got a little older, have taken me a lifetime to overcome and sort out.

During my early primary years I discovered sport and would play and compete in as many sports as I could. I was very competitive and sports days were my favourite days at school. I would much rather be out playing sport than sitting in the classroom. I developed a large group of friends through playing sport, all of whom stayed with me right through to high school. We were all very different with different backgrounds, different talents and different personalities. There were boys and girls but the one thing we had in common was sport.

By and large, I found my male friends easier to be with than my female friends. I am sure this was a consequence of being a bit of a tomboy and having three older brothers. I also realised very early in life how nasty and 'catty' some girls could be and, sadly, like so many people I was badly bullied throughout my school years by such girls. I was also teased at home, as many younger siblings are by their brothers and sisters.

For as long as I can remember, each year my family would pack up and make the annual pilgrimage to St Leonards on the Bellarine Peninsula. These were happy and carefree days which we all looked forward to – meeting up with other families each year. We went there because then, as now, my father loved to fish, so off to St Leonards we'd go. I can remember being fascinated by the ocean water. It was so clear and fresh and salty – very different to the river water I was used to swimming in. Having been brought up on the Murray and Campaspe rivers, I assumed that all water was brown and murky! Little did I know that many years later I would live just down the road from the holiday house we used to stay in.

During my childhood my paternal grandmother was an important influence on me as the matriarch of our family. She bred Labradors for the blind. I enjoyed going to stay with her and helping her with the dogs and puppies but more importantly I realise now how well organised and professional she was about the whole operation. This had a profound effect on me and I am grateful to her for that; even today her work ethic and standards are still with me. I can see now that I am very like her in many ways. I set in place high standards for my business and personal life and it is through her that I learnt this. She was typical of her generation with high moral standards, good manners and a strong work ethic which she expected others to live up to and emulate. I think she was the hardest, toughest woman I have ever met. Tough, fair and full of love − a rare combination. I have never lost my admiration for who she was and what she did. She never judged anyone, never had a bad word to say about anyone but got on with her life and her own business. Her family meant everything to her and she was kind and loving to us all. Fortunately she lived a long time which meant she and I had a good relationship for many years. She died when I was in my late thirties.

Some of my fondest childhood memories are of spending time with my grandmother, but also of the times my mother would take me with her to visit our elderly neighbors just as she does today. I'd sit and chatter with them for hours. I really enjoyed speaking with them and learning all about about their lives and a bygone era; it was fascinating and stimulating. Today I still love sitting with the elderly and listening to their stories and hearing all about their lives, their experiences, lapping up and listening to the wisdom they have gained over a lifetime.

I get excited when a woman over sixty-five comes to my camps because I love hearing about her life's journey.

I don't really remember the particular moment I came into contact with horses. My family was completely non-horsey except for my sister, who had the uncanny knack of turning up at home with the occasional new horse! (Whether she owned them or borrowed them I'll never know.) By late primary school I had started riding any horse I could get my hands on. I rode bareback all the time – there was no such thing as the luxury of a saddle and if I was lucky I sometimes had a bridle. Riding bareback with or without a bridle was a sure-fire way to learn how to stay on a horse! Sometimes I came off but like most kids I always managed to scramble back on come hell or high water.

One of the first lessons I recall in developing sheer dogged determination and guts was, ironically but not surprisingly, taught to me by a pint-sized Shetland. He was owned by the family who ran the local milk bar. They were happy for me to ride him as long as I could catch him (not an easy feat, as I was soon to discover) and return him to his paddock after riding him. He was a little black gelding around 10.2 hands high called Tiny (seems this is a common name for these little devils). After hours of perseverance I was finally successful in catching him; I then rode him back home, 3 kilometetres away, where I groomed him and spoiled him rotten with titbits, feeding him everything I could get my hands on. Afterwards I proceeded to ride him in the long railway paddock opposite our house. In typical Shetland fashion, when he believed he had done enough he would buck me off and belt back towards home at great speed! I did this without fail every day over many summer months. I never got frustrated, I was just so grateful I had a horse to ride. Tiny left an indelible mark on my memory; even though he is long gone, if I get a horse I cannot catch he is the first thing that jumps into my mind, the little bugger!

From the sublime to the ridiculous, my next love affair with a horse was a big, wide Percheron called Flash; he really didn't live up to his name because I don't think he ever got out of a walk. I don't recall him cantering or even trotting but if you accidentally dug your heels into his flank he'd pig-root or give a small buck, which would make me laugh. He had a long chain tether which he would drag behind him as we rode him bareback to school and back again. I never knew who owned him – he seemed to belong to the town because nearly everyone in town used Flash for one reason or another. He was around for about eight or ten years.

I figured out very early how to mount a horse that was too big for me. I would let the horse stand and graze; then while it was grazing I'd put its head between my knees and somehow the horse would flick me up onto its back. If this didn't work and there were two or more of us, the first rider would get on and hook their foot up and the others could use that to haul themselves up; we were, like most kids, quite ingenious in figuring out a way to get what we wanted. This is definitely not a method I would try or recommend today but I would like to be that agile again without a doubt!

Hardly any of the local horse-mad kids, including my sister and me, had any horse gear when we growing up as our parents had neither the money nor the inclination to spend it on these sorts of things; every piece of gear we did manage to acquire was borrowed. What we couldn't borrow we would make and my lifelong fondness of the majestic peppercorn tree came about because that's how I learnt to make whips. You ride up to a tree, pull off a branch, strip it of its leaves and that would become the whip to try to get that elusive trot from old Flash.

To my complete and utter amazement, one summer my sister came home with a saddle – from where I'll never know. I spent hours and hours sitting on it perched on the fence and I would pretend I was riding the world's most beautiful horse at a fast gallop. These games were so vivid to me and through them I began to understand that somehow I had to find a way to spend my life with horses.

Once I had discovered horses, school became the least favourite thing in my life. Horse riding and anything about horses took over my thoughts and became an addiction and passion. I soon sorted all the kids at school into who owned horses and who didn't. The ones who did became my best friends. Every weekend I would be invited to have a sleepover at one of their places. I was a sponge when it came to learning about horses and I wanted to spend as much time as I could with horses, no matter what the discipline. I was desperate for information from anyone who owned a horse.

When I was in grade six or seven I was offered my first horse as a lease. He was a pony; I'm not sure what breed he was but he was about 13 hands high. He lived on a dairy farm 10 kilometres away and I had no way of picking him up. I was not going to be deterred, however, so I decided to ride him home. The little incy wincy tiny detail that no-one bothered to tell me at the time was that he was a chronic rearer! If you have ever ridden a horse that reared and managed to stay on board then you will know that this was no mean feat! It was quite literally the ride of my life: ten steps forward, stop, rear, ten steps forward, stop, rear. I gritted my teeth and told myself that I would not fall off. I didn't, but what should have been a two-hour ride took close to eight hours. I don't think I have ever been so exhausted in my life.

I had that pony for over a year. The rearing soon became a thing of the past and there was nothing he wouldn't do for me in the end, which wasn't through good training (I was only a kid) but simply from riding him and handling him consistently. I woke up one morning to see him being loaded into a float by his owners and taken to Bendigo to be sold, and I never saw him again. I was heartbroken. At the time he was the closest thing I had to a possession of my very own. He gave me the freedom to go wherever I wanted around town and he became, as many ponies do for little girls, my friend and my confidante; he knew all my secrets that I whispered into his mane. When he was taken away I felt I had lost a very important part of my life. It was as if my autonomy had been taken away and loaded up onto that float with him.

Desperate to ride, I quickly got a reputation around town as the kid who would ride anything. I would jump on any horse or pony offered to me. Back then I didn't know the risks I was taking and even if I did I doubt I would have cared. If someone said 'Get on it and ride it' I'd get on and ride, whether it bucked, reared or bolted; all I cared about was having a horse to ride.

Horses became not only my friends but my mode of transport too. The distances I would travel around the district, often 'double-dinking' with someone else, were amazing. I would ride to other towns or out to water channels; I'd ride to visit my friends and even to the local footy. One of my fondest memories is of a local horse-breaker named Albie Godden. He was involved with horses all his life and what he didn't know about them wasn't worth knowing. Albie always had yards full of horses, mainly from the local Echuca horse sales. No matter what day we turned up he would always give us horses to ride. I would ride around town following him in his horse and cart. It was a common occurrence to see half a dozen or so kids meandering along behind his cart on a weekend. I now realise that we were an easy solution to get the miles on his young horses but the knowledge he gave me over the years and the experience I gained became invaluable and I will be forever grateful. Never was there a question – whether a horsey question or just a question about life in general – to which he didn't have an answer. The best piece of advice he ever gave me was 'When you get tossed off don't just sit there feeling sorry for yourself, pick yourself up and get back on!' I think this is a really good piece of advice for everyone, whether we are riders or not, and a good metaphor for life. After all what else are you going to do?

Albie was a real father figure to many of the children in town. He was an articulate gentleman, kind, fun-loving, engaging and he was never too busy for you. For many of the local children he provided a sense of stability that some didn't have in their families. I adored him and even though I was a friend of his daughter I was fonder of him and had a stronger relationship with him than I did with her.

My pre-teenage years were by and large fun-filled and uncomplicated. The one drama I seemed to constantly get caught up in was arriving home late from riding and having to face my father (but more on that later!). School continued to be a chore and this certainly didn't get any better once I started high school. I felt as if I only went to school to pass the time when I couldn't ride. I did the barest minimum that was required of me at school but that was all, unless it happened to be sport.

When I was around twelve or thirteen, I befriended a local girl called Caroline. I met Caroline at Albie Gooden's as she was horse mad just like me and hung off every word he said. Caroline was two years my senior and a lot more mature than I was but we clicked and became inseparable. We didn't know it at the time but our friendship was to become a lifelong one. Our journeys throughout life have often been parallel.

Luckily for me Caroline had lots of horses over the years, and good ones too. She always wanted someone to ride with so I was always guaranteed a ride. We both had a love of music and our taste was the same, and it was not unusual for us to be heard riding around town performing our rendition of Rod Stewart's latest album word for word. Our very favourite, 'Billy Don't be a Hero' by Paper Lace, soon became our anthem. Our friendship was very normal and innocent despite my parents' dislike of the age difference or the fact that Caroline went to another school. Our insistence on spending time together and to be best friends paid off and mostly we were left alone to explore the world (and Rochester was our world back then) with our ever-so-trusting four-legged modes of transport.

When I think today about what true friendship means to me, it is Caroline who always springs to mind. She knew everything about me and she never ever said anything negative about or to me. Oh sure, she would challenge me to make me better and she would tell me when I was wrong but she was always there, unconditionally. I get Christmas cards from her every year and if I'm home I'll go and visit her. Caroline is the funniest woman I know and suffers terribly from verbal diarrhoea – one of the many things I love about her. If we get together when David, my husband, is around he has to leave the room after about half an hour because he's so bombarded with all the chatter and laughter. He loves her too, though, and knows how much we have shared together and how important her friendship is to me. She is the one person in my life who has been with me through thick and thin and she has always had my back.

Caroline and I did all sorts of things together. She was the one who taught me how to smoke and drink – maybe not the best things to teach someone! She loved Ouzo and because of this I developed a taste for it too. It is still my drink of choice today. In regards to our passion for horses we just figured it out as we went along – it wasn't really 'horsemanship' it was just something we both enjoyed and discovered as our friendship grew. Our horse riding was just pure fun and we used it as our social outlet every weekend and every day after school. I got so carried away with this friendship and my obsession with horses that it led me into all sorts of trouble as a child. I would never get home when I was meant to and subsequently when it started to get dark my father would drive around town till he found me. In my eyes I wasn't doing anything wrong, but I wasn't home and my parents would be frantic with worry. I would go out riding because I had half an hour to spare and before you knew it three hours had flown past and I had lost track both of time and where I was meant to be – at home!

It was around this time that I learnt about my father's expectations of my behaviour and also about what would happen if I pushed the boundaries. There was to be *no* pushing of any boundaries my father put in place; he was very clear and he was very rigid about sticking to his rules no matter what. Many a time I would get an absolute flogging from my father for my 'disobedience' by arriving home late. As a result of this it didn't take me long to discover the dynamics that existed between my mother and father. My father was the disciplinarian of the family; there was no getting around him at all. There was no form of negotiation with him – when he said no he meant no. My mother was meek and mild in comparison. I don't know whether it was by choice or because of her upbringing, but either way she would never take on the disciplinarian role. When I heard the phrase 'You wait till your father gets home' I would quake with fear because I knew I was in deep trouble! I had seen him discipline my brothers and that used to scare me because he was very strong. He was never abusive but you'd cop a good bruise on your butt when he got you. At the time we never thought it was justified, but when I reflect back on it now I see that it really probably was justified for the things we got up to and our disrespect of the rules. I did deserve some form of punishment for my lack of consideration at the very least.

When I became a parent I found myself disciplining in the same way my father had and that took me aback. It was frightening. I stopped myself immediately as I was scared of my actions and the consequences they may have had. That style of parenting was long gone so I looked around me; I read some books and I started to copy other people's techniques in the hope that I would not inflict upon my children the negative things that had been inflicted upon me. My father would never listen or make any attempt to communicate with me or my other siblings. He never bothered to hear our side of the story over anything. Many a time I would be punished for something I didn't do but he did not want to know about it. It got to a point where the punishment wouldn't bother me but the injustice of receiving the punishment for something I hadn't done, did. I locked that piece of emotional memory away to deal with later in my life and because of this I have made it my business to listen as a parent (or at least I think I try!).

This was the era when you'd go out and play around the district and your parents wouldn't necessarily know exactly where you were. My parents may not have known where I was but they always knew who I was with: Caroline. In a small town it didn't really matter much where you were; there weren't many choices and you'd never be that far away. You were either at the footy or netball on a Saturday, or on Sunday you would be down at the irrigation channel or river swimming. There was a curfew you had to work to and if you didn't you were in trouble, as I found out time and time again.

Local dances were one of the highlights of the social calendar and Rochester was no different from any other country town in that regard. When I wanted to go to my first dance I had to beg, borrow and steal an outfit from my girlfriends and then try to convince my father to let me go. When he finally said yes I was only allowed to stay from 7 pm till 8.30 pm, but that was good enough for me. I was so excited because I felt pretty getting all frocked up. I never got any positive compliments from anyone in my family or any of my friends; about all anyone commented on was my curly hair and that was usually accompanied by someone pulling it! That dance was the last time I ever remember wearing a dress. I have only ever owned one dress apart from my wedding dress. I loved my wedding dress for what it represented but I didn't like wearing it. I don't really like wearing dresses at all but maybe that's what comes from being a tomboy. When I put on a dress I felt I had to behave in a way that was foreign to me and made me feel awkward and uncomfortable.

During this time my friendship with Caroline grew. She was fairly influential on my social outlook and interaction with our peers. Naturally it didn't take too long for our shared interests to include not only horses but the opposite sex. I figured out (to some extent) what boys and the opposite sex meant a lot earlier than I should have. I had no understanding, however, about adolescence or sexuality. In my mind sex is just another form of physical activity and I was totally unaware of what could and would be the consequences of this naive 'What does it matter?' mentality. I truly did not understand or even think about what would be the consequences of what I was doing with my boyfriend – that's right, at the tender age of thirteen I had a long-term boyfriend. We were dating and did everything that dating involved. Caroline also had a long-term relationship at the same time. I am still friends with her boyfriend from then to this very day.

Despite having a 'boyfriend' he played second fiddle to my love of horses. Caroline and I did, however, manage to incorporate meeting our boyfriends as part of the ten or twelve kids we'd hang out with – so typical of the social gathering of youngies in a small town. You can still see groups of young people doing the same thing if you go to small country towns. Unfortunately, though, it's now become unsafe for young people to be free and roam around together as we did.

Along with my friendship with Caroline came a new circle of friends who were all a bit older than I was and different to my friends at school. I found myself becoming quite a busy social butterfly flitting from the friends I had met through Caroline to my friends at school and also going out with all my brothers' and sister's friends too. Everyone ended up knowing everyone else.

All in all my life at this time seemed pretty normal and much like everyone else's I knew. In addition to enjoying my friends' company I poured every moment possible into horses and horse riding. My family was not picture perfect but I don't remember much of anything sad. I think my parents were typical of their generation and they had fairly typical family values. Today things are quite different and there is a big emphasis on families being close and parents making a conscious effort to develop a communicative and involved relationship with their children. Parents today seem intent on teaching their children everything they need to know to make the most of the opportunities in the world. For my parents' generation it seemed that couples just had a family because that was what was expected of them. There's a big difference between these two parenting techniques. Raising children back then seemed to be far simpler. There didn't appear to be so many rules and regulations about parenting, not so many things to think about or overthink and kids had far more personal and emotional freedom than they do today.

My siblings were getting older and starting out on their own as young adults; slowly I felt as if I was being left behind. I became very lonely at home without them and I lost the security of being part of a big family. I kept riding and spending time with Caroline which helped, and this sense of loss of family made me spend more and more time with her family. It was as if they had become mine too. I think I slept more at her place than my own over some of the holidays.

My world was soon to turn upside down. I didn't know it then but there was soon to be an event that would change my life completely.

Chapter 3

The teen years

Things started to change; the dynamics of my family started to shift. My siblings didn't have time for their younger sister and most of the time they were never home. My family as I knew it started to dissipate as my older brothers and sister went off to look for work. Inevitably a couple of them moved away to Melbourne. I soldiered on but it felt strange and unfamiliar and these changes made me feel more than a little insecure. Perhaps this is what happens to the youngest in a family as the older children leave home – in a way I got left behind and felt as if I had been forgotten. I think I was the only one who noticed the change in our family. I didn't like it, it felt weird.

One day my mother went into hospital for some routine surgery. She was away from home for quite a while. On the first night she was gone I was home on my own, though my father was meant to have been there too. That night I climbed into my parents' bed because it felt safe and while I was there I found a letter to my father under his pillow. It was not from my mother. I didn't fully understand its content but I had an overwhelming feeling that my mum needed to see it. When I woke up I knew this was not a safe secret to keep so I went straight to the hospital.

When I showed her the letter she became hysterical. I was removed by the nurses and taken to a waiting room where I was told to stay and not move. After a couple of hours I was taken to a friend's place. Eventually I remember my father coming up the driveway to collect me. I could have sworn if he'd had a gun he would have shot me. I didn't have a clue what was happening but it seemed as if I had done something very wrong and I was terrified.

I stayed with my friend until my mother got out of hospital. In the meantime Dad had apparently moved out of home. Everything unfolded on hearsay; no-one actually told me anything. I just heard through the grapevine that my father had left. I went back home to a very, very distraught, emotionally crushed and fragile mother. In the middle of all this chaos I was unable to understand what had happened and felt there was a distinct possibility it was all because of me and something I had done.

What I eventually found out was that the letter I had given to Mum was from a woman with whom my father had been having an affair. My parents' marriage was over. My mother had no idea about his infidelity, which is why it was such a devastating shock to her. She hadn't realised how bad things were between her and Dad and to be confronted out of the blue and at a time when she was vulnerable was almost more than she could cope with.

I don't know if Dad ever intended on leaving the marriage but I feel certain it would not have been in such an abrupt way. He was so angry with me and made me feel it was somehow all my fault. I suppose my actions had been the catalyst for the truth coming out.

My mother thought she had a stable, happy marriage and family then suddenly she had nothing. She lost her identity and what was left was an empty shell. Her life as she knew it was over. In those days there was a stigma surrounding divorce and so it wasn't talked about. I think she probably felt ashamed not only about the circumstances that ended her marriage but also about her divorce. I realise now how difficult it must have been for her and I admire and respect her for putting her life back together piece by piece.

Initially there wasn't a day I don't remember her crying. I was so upset seeing her like that and I didn't know how to help her. The only thing I thought I could do was do my very best to look after myself and not be a bother to her. Every day I got myself out of the house and to and from school. I didn't really like school. I started to play up and rebel, as so many teenagers do, and go against everything I knew I should be doing and started to do what I knew I shouldn't be.

Before my father left I would get into trouble if I wasn't home by 5.30 pm; now if I was at a friend's place till nine o'clock at night nobody seemed to know or care. I was too young to have no boundaries whatsoever but my mother was just hanging on herself. I felt very lost and alone and missed my family unit as I had known it.

I remember going to Melbourne from time to time on the bus to visit my siblings. Mum was happy to hand over the bus fare. I think she thought it would be good for me to see my sister and brothers and I'd be safe with them. I had other ideas and thought that maybe I could get a job too and have my own flat; that way I could be 'grown up' like them and be closer to them as well. However, they weren't all that interested in having their baby sister around. In fact I think one of them told me I was a 'pain in the arse'! I was barely fourteen years old but I was trying to behave like an adult.

My dislike for school became more like outright hate. I wondered what the hell I was there for. The routine of going to school and the expectations of your family are, I feel, what keeps most young people focused during that particular time of their life. I never had that focus or expectation. One of the teachers at school who also acted as a counsellor tried to help me but I was so angry and had so much aggression built up inside she could not get through to me, try as she might.

Not surprisingly I stopped going to school at all. Occasionally my mother would see me up the street on her way to work and say 'Why aren't you at school? Go to school Sandi.' My reply to that was 'Make me'.

Eventually my wayward behaviour meant that I found myself fourteen years old and pregnant. Yes, that's right fourteen years old and pregnant. The boy that I had been going out with was the father. I was so naïve and had been given no information whatsoever about 'the birds and the bees', I did not make the connection between having sex and having a baby. I had made the move to Melbourne by then and had found a job working in a pharmacy (I don't know if you were even legally allowed to work at that age but nobody ever questioned my age). I was sharing a little unit with a friend of my sister. One day a friend of mine came around to visit me a few days after I had moved in and wasn't able to find me. He knew I was at home because we had spoken earlier so when he couldn't find me he broke into the unit. I had collapsed and he found me semi-conscious on the bathroom floor.

He picked me up and took me to hospital. I had gone into renal failure after having been sick for quite some time, unaware I was pregnant and just thinking it was something I would get over. When I regained consciousness I was very, very ill. To make matters worse both my parents were in the room when I awoke and this really frightened me as I had not seen my father since he left. I knew that if they were both there together it must be really serious. Mum must have rung Dad when the hospital contacted her as my next of kin; that would have been an incredibly difficult thing for her to do but it showed the magnitude and seriousness of my predicament. My father stood at the end of the bed, outraged. 'Who is the bastard?' he yelled. 'If I catch him I'll kill him!' I was in utter shock and disbelief when first told I was pregnant. 'I'm what?' I asked. They told me again that I was seven months pregnant and it took me a good week to process it. I had no idea that I was pregnant, no idea at all. I wasn't really even that fat, I was a beanpole.

After I was discharged from hospital I was sent to a home for pregnant teenagers, or 'wayward girls', in the Melbourne suburb of Kew.

For the rest of my pregnancy I lived with about thirty other girls. Some were from very wealthy families, some were from poor families, some had drug issues, some had alcohol issues and I was right in the midst of all of them. There were a few country girls and I was one of those few. I hated the home, but looking back now I am thankful I had that place to go to – who knows where I would have ended up. I didn't have any other options. All of my rights were taken away because I was so young. I don't remember anything bad about that place but I also don't remember anything that was all that good. I do know I was well cared for medically, I ate three meals a day and I was around other girls who were as big as I was with their pregnancies. We swapped and changed clothes and chatted a lot so there was some companionship with others in the same predicament. As far as having any real understanding that I was about to have a baby, well I just didn't; it didn't even really make any sense to me that I was about to have a child apart from the fact that I couldn't fit into my clothes.

The sex education talk most children get when they're growing up hadn't happened for me; that was when my family fell apart and other things took priority. Caroline was the only one who helped me out when I started getting my periods and it was very basic and brief! She just said 'You use these' and handed me a tampon and I said 'Thanks, where do you put it?' It was also in a day and age where 'those' things weren't spoken of nearly as much as they are today. For me they weren't spoken of at all and that's a conversation which could have dramatically changed my life.

I didn't get any visitors other than my mum and sometimes my sister, but when they came it would just be to talk about what a lovely day it was and things like that. My 'situation' wasn't discussed or even referred to; it was as if it wasn't happening. I don't think for a second that my mother ever stopped loving me. I would never say that about her; I know that she's always done the best she could. I just don't think she knew what to do and so a lot went unsaid.

Every morning at about quarter past nine at the home, I had a session with someone who was a 'therapist' or counsellor or something like that. She would try to get me to understand what was happening to me and then she would push some papers under my nose and say, 'Just sign here'. She did that for around six to eight weeks every day, 'Just sign here'. I was so frightened to sign that piece of paper. Even though I was legally a minor it was *my* signature that was required on the documentation. I didn't know why they wanted me to sign, all I was concerned about was that I didn't know how to sign my name. I'd never been asked to sign my name so I refused to do it not because of the papers or what they meant but because I didn't want to look like a fool! I made sure as a result of this that as soon as my children learnt how to write they learnt how to sign their name. Even today this is still loud and clear in my memory as I felt really intimidated.

What I didn't know at the time was that they were adoption papers.

My mother was required to countersign as my legal guardian but the baby could not be adopted out without my permission, no matter what any adult wanted. They were all trying desperately to get me to sign the adoption papers and to then take my child. I didn't really understand what they were talking to me about, I just thought we were having a chat each time we met. Who understands therapy or counselling at that age?

During my stay at the home they were asking for volunteers to enter into a study of some sort on teenage pregnancies. 'Why not?' I thought, it was something to do and why wouldn't I do it? I formed quite a good friendship with the nurse who collected all the information when she came each week. During these weekly visits she would take my blood pressure, monitor the baby's heart rate and take blood for pathology. I felt empowered by being part of this 'experiment' for the greater good. Superficially the nurse became an important part of my life in that home and so were her weekly visits, which were the one constant in my life. She made me feel good about myself and what I was doing. Not too many people had ever made me feel that way throughout my life so her friendship was unusual and extremely important to me even though it was a short-term one.

I talked to the other girls in the home. Some had chosen to keep their babies while others had chosen to put them up for adoption, but back then adoption was very secretive. It was only after speaking to the other girls that I finally got a clue about the avenues of action I could take. When I thought about giving away my child it was just never an option for me. It was part of the very core of me even at that age. My attitude was that, if this came out of me it was mine and it was not for anyone else to have. It wasn't even a decision; it was just instinctive. All of a sudden I said to myself, 'Well if I don't have my family anymore, I'll create my own.'

I started replacing my lost family with images of my own family – me and my baby – and in my mind everything was going to be fine. I'd have the baby and everything would be great. Before she was born (and yes, the baby was a girl according to me) I had named her and bought all of her clothes. I think I wanted a girl so badly because I had been brought up with so many boys and had been emotionally scarred by most of the men in my life. I did all the stuff to create the fantasy of being a parent but I couldn't have been more underprepared. The only thing I knew for sure and with complete and utter conviction was that the baby was mine and mine alone and she and I would create our own happy family. My mind was made up and I wasn't going to be persuaded to do anything else. I grew more and more determined. Nobody was going to take me off my chosen path. I learnt to say no. I wouldn't even entertain anyone else's ideas or opinions. I just learnt to say, 'No, I'm doing it this way!' Sometimes my stubborn streak had worked against me but in this instance I made it work for me.

My beautiful daughter arrived (and yes she was a girl!) after a gruelling 36-hour labor. Due to the length of the labour she went into foetal distress three times. I was told by the medical staff that it was because I was too small and young to be having a child. There was no-one from my family with me at the birth. The mother of one of my friends from the home volunteered to come with me, bless her. I was so grateful to her for helping me at that very difficult time. The birth was horrific. I had never experienced so much pain in my life and I felt like it would never end. How could I ever be the same or recover from this agony? I was simply too young to be going through this on my own without any mental preparation or emotional support from people I knew and trusted. When it was finally over I remember they handed my daughter to me to breastfeed and I said, 'Oh I don't think so, there'll be none of that' because I was too immature to think that anyone should touch my body, even my own child. I told them we were bottle-feeding thank you!

While my daughter and I lay in the hospital and recovered from our ordeal I wondered about what was going to happen next. I was terrified, emotional and overwhelmed.

Chapter 4

Motherhood

When it was time to leave the hospital I certainly wasn't in any hurry to go. In hospital I had a support network around me and a routine, with people who could help and advise me twenty-four hours a day if I needed them. I was told how to change my baby's nappy when it was wet or dirty and that I needed to feed her every four hours religiously at two, six, ten, two, six, ten and that was about it!

I was eventually discharged when my baby was five days old. There I was with my tiny newborn daughter, on the horns of a dilemma from the very onset as no-one from my family was able to come and pick us up. It was difficult going back home with my daughter. It was absolutely scandalous for a fourteen-year-old girl to be pregnant and keep her baby in the early 1970s in rural Australia. There was no such thing as a 'legal abortion' and some girls would just disappear from the area during their pregnancy, as I did, and were not spoken about again. I didn't know I was pregnant until I was seven months so terminating the pregnancy was not an option. In all honesty I am pretty sure I would not have chosen that option anyway even if I had found out earlier.

Eventually, my baby daughter and I were picked up from the hospital in Melbourne by Caroline's boyfriend. He had just become a father himself a few days before. Fancy that, my best friend Caroline had become pregnant and had a child, a son, at the same time as me. What were the chances of that happening? At the time we thought it was quite amazing; we still to this very day feel this way. The boy who got me pregnant was never made accountable. He never knew until much later on that he had a daughter but he had no interest whatsoever and that's okay because it wasn't about him and it wasn't about any sort of meaningful, long-term relationship; we were only kids ourselves.

My best friend was in the same boat dealing with the same issues and challenges as I was. I felt better about my plight because Caroline was doing what I was doing. She had been able to stay in town because the boy who got her pregnant knew about it and their son. The fact that she was two years older than me also made the situation a bit more respectable and acceptable. Her family gave her all the care and emotional support she needed – I was really happy for her and her son. I was also a tiny bit envious and, yes, at times jealous. I was in a very different position at the time due to the breakdown of my family unit; even if they had wanted to rally around and support me they weren't able to do so. My family was the complete antithesis of Caroline's family, who was close knit, non-judgemental and supportive of one another no matter what. It was these characteristics that enabled her to be nurtured and supported.

My mother, bless her heart, took us into her home with open arms and proceeded to become the most amazing grandparent to her new baby granddaughter. By this stage she had started to slowly recover from her marriage break-up with the support and love of the people of Rochester. My mother tells the story of how not long after my father left there was a knock at the front door. When she opened it, standing there was the matron of the hospital wondering if Mum would like a job as a cook. My mother jumped at the chance. She knew she had to earn money to support herself and she loved cooking. She worked there for many years and was able to get her formal chef certification, something of which she is tremendously proud, as well she should be. She also asked her brother-in-law to teach her to drive so she could get her licence. This was no mean feat for a 'mature age' lady. Once she had her licence, her father bought her her first car. I really admire her for having the courage and tenacity to turn her life around in such a positive way. She was a wonderful role model for me later on in life when I had grown up a bit and needed to take stock of who I was and where I was at.

When I was living with her on my return to Rochester she even found the courage to go on the occasional date. I found the fact that my mother would go out with a man other than my father really intimidating. Instead of my father being in the house there would be another man there, which threw me into a real spin. She has now been happily married to this man for over thirty years. I am so happy for her to have found someone to love and look after her and she him, but back when I was trying to sort myself out and adjust to being a parent myself I found my mother's new relationship a little difficult to come to terms with.

Unable to deal with all the changes going on around me and within me, my anger reached new heights and so began another emotional battle. The attitude in town towards me being a single parent was fairly ambivalent. People felt awkward and treated me with a type of polite disdain. I felt uncomfortable and insecure. I already disliked myself enough without any added burden and I felt I was living my life in shame for being a teenage mother. It got to the point where I built a protective veneer around myself. I would not and could not allow myself to be hurt emotionally or taken advantage of. I had to get on with my life and look after my daughter, my number one priority.

My darling daughter was a great little kid. She still is, although she is hardly a kid any more, being over thirty. I adore her and I cannot tell you how proud I am of her. When she was growing up I made sure she knew all about the birds and the bees and the consequences of her actions in all aspects of her life – physically, emotionally and morally. She was a good pupil and/or I was a good teacher (fancy that!) and is one of the most together, well-balanced young women you will ever have the pleasure of meeting. With all my children I tried to make sure I kept no stone unturned about 'life' and I endeavoured to give them all sorts of information about all sorts of things. I want them to be well informed about as many things as possible so that they can make mature and responsible decisions. Everything that I could think of was talked about and discussed.

Above all I told them to love themselves, be proud of who they are, and be respectful towards others and themselves.

When I returned home it became obvious to me that I didn't fit in anywhere. My school friends were still at school. The only place I did fit in was with Caroline. Had Caroline not been in the same boat as I was there certainly would have been a different outcome. She kept reminding me that it was okay to be a parent at this age. 'We can do this!' she would constantly say. Her son was a gorgeous baby but he was a challenge for a young mum when he was little, being colicky and unsettled.

Luckily for me my daughter would sit in the pusher all day and I wouldn't hear a peep from her. By and large she was a passive baby and child but she was constantly sick from birth onwards and was in and out of hospital. I was reported to child welfare for being a bad parent because of her many hospital stays. Can you imagine? A teenage mother appearing at the local hospital with a sick baby time after time. She would be stabilised at hospital, sent home and then almost immediately become sick again and have to go back to hospital. I felt an enormous amount of guilt when she was sick and didn't go to visit her in hospital. The hospital staff would ring my mother and she would tell me when it was time to go and pick her up.

Eventually after quite a few admissions a more enlightened doctor discovered she had lactose intolerance and was allergic to all dairy products, including the formula I had been feeding her. No wonder she got sick as soon as she came home! But the stress I went through because my child was unwell and needed repeat visits to hospital was enormous. I was always on the defensive and any guilt I experienced turned to anger in a heartbeat if I felt I was cornered and challenged in any way about my parenting.

My daughter and I continued to live with my mother for a couple of months although I endeavoured to move out several times. I wanted to be an adult and live like an adult – after all, I was a mother so it was time for me to grow up and be responsible. Inevitably I found that it was a steep learning curve when I moved out. I had no idea how to go about paying bills, how to budget or how to run a home. I had no knowledge about what needed to be done nor how to do it. Occasionally my sister would visit and try to help but I had become so doggedly determined to be independent that I stubbornly refused to listen and told her I didn't need any help.

I muddled through life the best way I could for a while until one day I met a young man who I thought at the time was the love of my life. He was the 'boy next door'. I was so pleased I had found someone who thought I was pretty okay and wanted to spend time with me. We started to go out together and one thing led to another. At the ripe old age of sixteen I was pregnant again but unlike last time I was older and in a steady relationship with the father of the baby, and he was going to stick around by the looks of things. There was a lot of pressure on us to 'do the right thing' and get married, and so we did.

Chapter 5

Marriage

I felt convinced that getting married was the right thing to do because then I would feel 'normal' and be like everyone else. I wore a borrowed dress to our wedding. I was four months pregnant and the reception was a barbecue in the backyard of my mother's house. My mother refused to come to the wedding or the reception even though it was in her own home because my father was going to be there. She still wasn't able to cope with seeing him and having old memories dredged up. It wasn't a wedding as you would expect; it was really just a big party. When everyone eventually left they went into town to party on. I couldn't go because I was pregnant but my new husband did and he spent our wedding night in jail as he got into a brawl. It was a sad indictment of things to come.

When I went to hospital to have our son my husband was nowhere to be found. He turned up the next day, walked into the hospital and simply said, 'Well where is it?' He didn't know whether he had a son or daughter and I was horrified by the perfunctory and flippant welcome he gave our son. Even though this time I was married I got the distinct impression that, again, I was going to be alone during motherhood. Sadly, my dream of having a happy family and the white picket fence were evidently not to become reality.

I don't think any part of that time in my life was really happy. The dysfunction of our marriage (if that's what you could call it) became more and more apparent and things went from bad to worse. He would disappear for days on end. I am sure people must have had an inkling about what was going on but they didn't talk about things like that back then; I was surrounded by silence. I have often wondered whether people saw the desolation in my eyes or even knew what was going on in our home and chose to ignore it. I have seen that look in people's eyes with the work I do today with women and their horses, and I will not ignore it because I know that reaching out, and offering kindness and a willing heart to listen with empathy and understanding, can make all the difference.

We lived in the same house but I didn't feel married, whatever that meant, and even though I hadn't been in this position before something deep down inside me felt as if I didn't really love him. I came to realise that we had only married because it was expected of us and I had wanted to do the right thing and desperately wanted everyone else's approval by doing so.

I lost count of the many times my husband was not at home when I needed him to help with the children. I was raising them on my own and when he was around he could be very distant and remote. The constant strain took its toll. One day I felt the situation had become so bad I went to my mother for help. 'Enough is enough Sandi,' she said. 'This is not the way to live your life nor is it fair to your children to be witness to what is happening to you.' I went to court to file for a restraining order with my two children in tow but the judge peered down his bespectacled face at me, told me to be a better wife and sent me home. How very enlightened of him! When I had recovered from the shock of his patriarchal attitude I decided to bide my time for a while and plot my course as to how I could manage to leave with my children to make a better life for us.

As fate would have it, my husband gave me the best set of parents-in-law anyone could ever wish for. They were to become very influential in my life; they were so kind and made sure they had constant contact with their grandchildren. I feel nothing but love and respect for them today as I did then because they are good, genuine people. They did their very best to give me as much support as possible. My husband was young and foolish like so many young men of that age who seem to think they are infallible and invincible. He seemed to be on a path of self-destruction. I think in our own immature way we were really trying to do the right thing at the beginning, but we just rolled from one emotional catastrophe to another.

There were times when, out of desperation, I would go and find my eldest brother when he was home from Geraldton and talk to him about my predicament. He always listened but, to my horror, one day he thought he would take matters into his own hands and went to talk to my husband. Feeling pleased with himself he came back to me and

said, 'You're right now, I've sorted it all out with him.' Little did he
know that when my husband got home that night he was angrier than I
had ever seen him – it was not a good night.

Sadly, at one point when I was still in Rochester things got so bad that
I put both my children into a foster home in Bendigo, with the help of
my mother. It was her idea, as she saw how overwhelmed and fragile I was
and realised that I needed a reprieve from being a mother and time to sort
out my situation without the added responsibility of the children.

My mother came over to my house one Sunday after she had received
an SOS from me. I remember it vividly. I was on the verge of a
breakdown. I had watched all of my friends getting on with their lives
and having fun as teenagers do, but here I was changing nappies and
battling on alone for the most part while my husband would disappear
and be of no help whatsoever. I felt as if my life was flying past me and
I was spiralling out of control. I told Mum that I couldn't do it anymore,
I hated not being able to have my own time, I hated not being free. I
wanted to be a parent but I didn't know how to deal with it. The only
solution my mother and I could come up with was to look into the
possibility of putting the children into foster care temporarily so I could
sort myself out. The children went into temporary foster care with a
wonderful family for three months.

At no time did I consider this would be anything more than a short-
term arrangement. It was merely an opportunity to ensure they had
security, stability and a routine with a loving family. I then had the
opportunity to do a lot of soul searching and to figure out how I was

going to get on with my life. I also took this opportunity to go out and have a little fun, like most seventeen-year-olds, while weighing up my options. My husband was gone all of that time so I had the space I needed. Boy, did I do some soul searching. I visited my children in Bendigo every Sunday with Mum. We'd take them to the lake in Bendigo, and I sat there and asked myself if I wanted the children and wanted to be a parent to them. It was an extremely challenging, emotional time. Mum was great; she would mind the children and wouldn't cross-examine me or question me while I sat there asking myself if I could do this and whether or not there was enough of me to go around. I kept coming to the same conclusion: yes I could do it and yes I did want my children. I wanted to be a wonderful parent in every sense of the word. I just didn't know where to start.

After three agonising months of questioning and digging deep I eventually figured it out. I knew I had to get out of Rochester and my marriage. I took my children out of foster care one at a time. They were just tots and didn't know any different so I don't think it left any scars; I hope not, but it certainly left one with me.

Mum and I kept that foster episode fairly quiet because Mum knew I'd had enough. She saw that in my face. It was at that point that it got hard, really hard but I don't think I ever thought of suicide or self-harm because I was a parent and I always knew that taking the easy way out was never an option. I was never going to give up on my children. I had to keep trying; whether that trying was to give them to someone else to raise because I couldn't or whether I had to figure out how to raise them better, I had to try.

My decision to leave was validated on the day when my husband's anger reached such an intangible and irrational level that I felt if he'd had a gun he would have used it. The very thought of this and the tenuousness of his mental state scared the living daylights out of me. I wasn't sure how or when but I knew I had to sit and wait and plan so that when I got away I would never have to come back to live with him again.

Over the next few months, as the situation at home went from bad to worse, I waited for the opportune moment to put my plan in place. My plan wasn't very complex by any stretch of the imagination – it was quite simply to pack myself and my children up and leave my husband behind. I knew I had to get away as far as possible as quickly as possible without arousing any suspicion. Over the weeks I was able to set aside a little bit of money for petrol and food for our escape without him realising and I put some feelers out as to where we might go when we left. Melbourne was where I imagined we would head – a big city where I could find accommodation and work and would be hard to find on the off chance he might come looking for us. I was terrified to tell anyone of my intentions as I didn't want my husband to find out. One thing I did know was that there was more to life than what I was currently experiencing and I wanted to go out and find out what it was. I didn't know what it was I was feeling – and I didn't know that it was to become one of the most fundamental parts of my character, one which would enable me to make decisions and overcome adversity throughout my life – but I recognise and appreciate now that women have an innate sense of how things should be and how to put things right. It is an intrinsic part of our female make-up and that's what makes us the nurturers and caregivers. My female intuition had been on high alert for some time to the gravity of the situation my children and I were in, and it was time to act.

One day the opportunity to leave presented itself. My husband was in one of his once-in-every-six months good moods. He went off that morning with an 'Okay honey, I'm off to the footy'. 'Okay,' I said and after he left I packed the car and left town with my children and the little bit of money I had managed to save. I remember the feeling of relief and elation as the miles rolled behind us. I felt liberated and freed from a terrible darkness that had been looming over me for so very long. I knew I was never going back to him and I never did. Such was my mindset I did not look back emotionally either. Naturally, I would revisit things in my mind from time to time but I never went back in any way, shape or form to revisit any aspect of my marriage.

We didn't get divorced for years but I couldn't have cared less. Upon reflection our marriage was doomed to failure from the very outset. The fact that I didn't need to go over the various aspects of it when I left enabled me to start afresh and put it all behind me without feeling any guilt or carrying any emotional baggage. I also began to appreciate another part of myself through all of this; I finally knew that if I ended up in the gutter I would keep on trying to get out and I would succeed.

Leaving all my troubles behind was empowering even though I didn't know exactly where I was going. But I wasn't staying where I had been, that's for sure!

Chapter 6

Starting to sort it out

Now that I had put some physical space between me and my disaster of a marriage I was able to start figuring out what I was to do next and how I would get there. I also had the time and space to start putting some work into myself and who I wanted to be as a young, single mother of two small children. I had to put myself first; my life became about me and what was best for me and the children.

I ended up living with a beautiful family in Melbourne, the Robinsons. I knew them from when they came to Rochester on holidays. Dulcie, the mother of the family, was a beautiful soul. She was a godsend and loved me and my children unconditionally, welcoming us into her home with open, non-judgemental arms. Through their love and support they showed me it was okay to be a young mum. I was given a wonderful opportunity to settle, take care of my kids and sort myself out. Dulcie looked after, guided and nurtured me for a long time and helped me to be become a good parent. She showed me the importance of a routine for the children and how to cook and care for them as she had done for her own family.

Ironically, the Robinsons lived around the corner from my in-laws and even though I was there for a year my husband never came after me or tried to find me. I don't know why he didn't. He must have known where we were – maybe it was too much trouble or perhaps he too was relieved the marriage was over. All I cared about was that he was finally out of the picture.

While I was living with the Robinsons I was able to try my hand at different things workwise and personally. I even started dating again, which more often than not went terribly wrong. I had an uncanny knack of picking the wrong men. Over the years I have seen a lot of women who seem to be cursed with this unfortunate attribute too! At that particular time in my life I was certainly one of them. In my defence even though I'd had a lot of things thrown at me in my short life I was still only a teenager with a teenager's brain. My one ambition at that time was to find that elusive state of 'normality'. The big problem with this was I didn't know what normality was.

After many attempts it became evident that, being such a young mother and trying to form a relationship with someone around my age who was going to accept me and my children, would be quite a challenge. Try having a date but having to be home by ten because the baby has to have a bottle! Dulcie and her family continued to give me unconditional support and I learnt what it means for someone to 'have your back'; if I was home late or wanted to go somewhere Dulcie, or

Ma Robbo as the children and I used to call her, would say to me, 'It's all right honey, I'm here with the kids, it's all right.' There were never any strings attached or any sense of being indebted to her. I think in all honesty we helped her, too. It was as if we were a breath of fresh air to her. She rang me a couple of years ago and although I hadn't heard from her in such a long time she said, 'And how's my gorgeous girl going?' It meant the world to me. Her own two children were both wonderful people and have families of their own now. Sadly I have lost contact with Dulcie but I feel pretty sure that my children and I still hold a special place in her heart – she certainly does in ours. I don't know what I would have done without her.

Later on that year I received some life changing and devastating news. My eldest brother had died in a car accident in New Zealand. When I heard the news I was overcome with gut-wrenching grief; this was completely unchartered emotional territory for me.

He was buried on my twenty-first birthday. After his funeral no-one in my family wanted to talk about what had happened. Unable to deal with their own grief, no-one would talk to me and tell me the details of the accident. I wanted to know. I needed to know, to get some grip on it. For his twin (my only sister) it was the beginning of a very dark time in her life. I don't think she has ever really gotten over it or accepted that she has lost him forever.

The community of Rochester came together to support my mother and the family. They quietly went about providing all the food and took care of all of the hospitality arrangements after the service. When there is a tragedy in such a small, close knit community it is as if the town itself extends its arms around its citizens and holds onto them, offering protection and solace in their hour of grief. Rochester was no different.

Even though my life was all over the place I did manage to start making some positive decisions (along with some not so positive). The constant support and gentle direction I received from the Robinson family and my in-laws kept me trying to move forward and make something of my life for my own sake and for my children. All along there was that inner conviction and belief that I knew I was better than what I had experienced up until then. I kept telling myself that it wasn't a bad thing to have two children at this age; it was just the way it was and I had to deal with it.

Parenting wasn't something that came naturally to me. I didn't have a handle on how to be a good parent in the sense of what to do and what not to do as far as discipline was concerned.

Years later when I reflected on some of my behaviour, I realised I had probably developed postnatal depression after my second child. It remained undiagnosed. Nobody ever asked me whether there was something more than just a young mother feeling stressed about coping on her own with two small children. I think I struggled on with postnatal depression for years and years, and I never knew what it was until I saw my sister suffering from it and recognised that that was what had happened to me. Young mothers today have so many resources and information available to them and while it is a terrible thing to have there is now better support and a greater understanding of the 'baby blues'. When I was having my babies it wasn't really understood or talked about and young mothers like me had two options: give up your children for adoption and never see them again or keep them.

One of my favorite television shows now is *Sixteen and pregnant* because I love seeing the evolution of support available medically and socially for these young girls. They are no longer judged for being teen mums. People are supporting these young girls and reinforcing to them that they have choices. Some schools even have daycare centres so that young mums can continue with their education. Nobody ever came to me and told me I could finish school. The fact that I was pregnant meant my schooling years were over.

When I was growing up I was loaned out as a babysitter to my parents' friends quite often. I was probably around the age of ten or twelve at the time. It was during this time that I began to realise I wasn't all that interested in children. There was not one inkling of a maternal instinct in my bones and children weren't something I saw in my future. I dreamed of travelling, being independent, free and strong. Someone who was able to make their own decisions, live by their own rules and be in complete control of their life. I didn't want the responsibility and I didn't have the instinct to nurture and care for another. It all seemed too complicated, confronting and too much like hard work.

I was astounded and confronted when I actually became a mother because of my non-maternal feelings. I found bonding with my baby really hard. I felt as if being a mother was the complete antithesis of who I wanted to be and what I wanted to do. I had a never-ending internal argument with myself and found I was in a state of constant turmoil and conflict about the way my life had turned out. My internal dialogue went something like this:

'I'm doing it but I don't like it.'

'But you should like it because they're yours. You're meant to love them.'

'Are you meant to love them? Really?'

Once you give birth, you know you wouldn't change a thing in a million years and I certainly was the same. I now believe the opposite to what I believed all those years ago. I believe I was put on this earth to have those children even though it was never something I saw myself doing. How ironic, though, to think that I didn't want children and now I have five.

I talk to a lot of women today who feel the same way I did. They ask these same questions: Should I even be a mother? Am I doing a good enough job? Am I able to offer them enough? They feel guilty for asking the questions and even feel guilty for having had children when perhaps they really didn't want to but felt it was expected of them. There are also women who don't want children and choose not to have any but at the same time feel guilty about not wanting to be a mother. I think it is perfectly normal to think and feel these things and I think we should bring these issues out into the open and be more honest about the fact that this is all a normal part of being a woman. There's just way too much hidden guilt that too many women carry around with them.

After my move to Melbourne and my year with the Robinsons I eventually moved to Geelong and proceeded to make another one hundred mistakes! It was very clear to me that I had to be a good parent and that meant looking after my children and earning money to raise them well. I did not want to be reliant on anyone except myself. I have never taken a cent of child support from anyone, even to this day. The children were mine and were my responsibility to care for, and so I did. I believe that was one of the most successful decisions of my life.

I managed to survive by working hard and that's pretty much all I ever did. I worked hard to raise my kids, made sure we had a roof over our heads and decent clothes and food on the table. I made sure never to be caught with my pants down and by that I mean never to be caught with a dirty faced child, a nappy that smelled, to always have a clean car and always have our house clean. I had battled the preconceived ideas of people who assumed I was a bad mother because I was young and single. The stigma and prejudice that had been levelled at me made me feel I had done everything wrong and it meant that I got to the point of saying, 'I'll prove you all wrong!'

Somewhere along the way I began to recognise that I had been playing the role of victim in my own life. It is quite a wake-up call when the penny drops and we realise that maybe we are allowing ourselves to operate as a victim rather than standing up, being accountable and taking control of our lives. I see this a lot nowadays in my work. It hits me between the eyes because I recognise the warning signs. It took me a long time to stop playing the victim and start being a survivor. Victim was the only role I knew. I didn't understand how dysfunctional I had become until it was pointed out to me later in life. When you see yourself as a victim it's always everyone else's fault, never your own; the 'poor me syndrome'. You don't own any of your mistakes. Nothing is ever your responsibility.

After I had been living in Geelong for a couple of years, I met a man who I thought at the time could have been 'the one'. I spent many years with him. Our relationship was a lot better than any other I had experienced. He was the first man who ever looked at me and cared about the way I looked. He would actually buy me some nice clothes to wear, give them to me and say, 'You'd look much nicer in that'. He was the first person who ever took me out for a meal – I was the mother of two children and still had never been taken out to dinner – and when he did he was a real gentleman. He really knew how to treat a woman well and I'll be forever grateful for that. He was and is a good man and he is still a good friend of mine.

We became engaged. I saw I had a life with him – a whole life with him. His parents did their best to accept me – I'm pretty sure it was not an ideal relationship in their eyes but it was okay. I was working hard and he was working hard and a few years into our engagement I found out I was pregnant. We had planned to have children so it wasn't a big deal, or so I thought. I remember sitting in the kitchen one day with his parents and telling them, 'By the way, the wedding date we have chosen might not work because I think I might be in labour that day!'

To my utter shock and surprise, when I told him he left so fast he nearly tore the door off its hinges. He couldn't have left any quicker. He was gone in an instant! I was gobsmacked by his extreme panic and reaction – I had certainly read that one wrong. All of a sudden I found myself on my own again with one child at school, one in kindergarten and pregnant with my next.

I was in shock but I also felt that familiar sense of hopelessness in the pit of my stomach; here I go again. So what did I do? What could I do but come up with exactly the same equation as before: I'd do this on my own. Again. I'd done it before so I knew I could do it again and that was that.

I loved him (well, what I thought at the time was love) and I told myself that if I couldn't have him, I'd have his child. We'd spent a lot of years together; it wasn't a fleeting relationship nor was it a dysfunctional one, not from my point of view anyway. It was as good and loving a relationship as I had ever experienced. After he walked out I tried to rekindle our relationship many times because I did think it was love and so it was worth giving it a go. As time went on, though, I eventually saw it for what it was. He was very controlling; he controlled me, he controlled the kids, and he saw us as trying to control his life. I think a lot of the reason for this was that he was busy trying to live up to the expectations of his family. His family was very important to him; at times I think they took priority over my needs and expectations.

I realise now, years later and in a happy and fulfilling relationship with my husband David, that the relationship I thought was love wasn't even close. Love is something far more complete, enveloping and greater than what we ever had. I believe true, lasting love is found in one another's actions and attitude. It is based on attraction, yes, but also a deep and abiding respect and commitment to one another without the need to change or manipulate the one you love. It can be expressed in a myriad of ways – thoughtfulness, tenderness, actions and reactions through all the ups and downs that life can present as individuals and as a couple. This relationship had none of these attributes. It had no depth and very little meaning. I thought I had found the right one and I felt validated by this. I'd go home to my mother and my friends and say, 'Look, I'm engaged!' and they seemed to be happy. Their happiness and acceptance was really important to me at this point in my life while I was still struggling to find my identity and my place in the scheme of things. When I eventually took my fiancé home to Rochester to introduce him to my mother and friends, my mother's female intuition kicked in and she took me aside and said, 'Sandi, I don't mean to interfere but I feel that this is not the right decision for you and your children. I can't put my finger on it but it just doesn't feel right.' The prophecy of her words was proven to be correct.

I gave birth to my third child, a son, some months later. I was close to my due date and living on my own again with a tiny bit of money I had saved and a little bit more my ex fiancé contributed at my insistence (it was his baby after all), which enabled me to at least go to a private hospital and choose my own doctor. However, the money did not stretch far enough to have any stay in hospital nor any of the usual postnatal care. When I did go into labour it was kind of a walk-in walk-out affair! My son was only six hours old when I left hospital armed with a bucketload of determination and the knowledge that I could make this work.

Once our son was born his father and I did attempt to make our relationship work. It was important to me try to resurrect it. I didn't want it to fail like every other relationship I had been in.

My fiancé and I muddled along trying to restore our relationship and look after our son, and it wasn't too long before I discovered I was pregnant again. Sadly, though, this pregnancy came to an end with a miscarriage. I spent Christmas Day that year in hospital miscarrying. It was to become one of the most life-changing days of my life.

At the time of my brother's death I thought that I could not feel anything worse than the grief associated with his loss. He was the last father figure I had ever known. I soon learnt that the grief I felt in his death could only be matched by that felt with the loss of my baby. I went through exactly what my mother went through when she lost her son in that car accident, only I didn't have my child for twenty-something years as my mother had, I had her for twenty-something minutes. There are now wonderful organisations such as SANDS and SIDS to offer help and counselling for parents who have tragically lost their babies through miscarriages, foetal death in utero and cot death. I know many women who have for many years carried the burden of grief from the loss of a child and they are able to find some comfort and solace through the services of these wonderful organisations staffed by men and women who have endured the same heartbreak.

I lay in the hospital bed after having just lost my baby, immersed in deep sorrow for the loss of a child I would never get to hold. My thoughts were broken by a kerfuffle outside in the hall. There were a whole lot of people yelling. My fiancé and his family had arrived at the hospital when they had learnt what had happened. He apparently refused to come in and see me and in all the noise I heard his mother say, 'If this is your child you're going to hell for this.' As I lay listening to this outburst I realised I was the only one who was ever going to grieve for that baby.

My children went and stayed with my mum and my fiance's family. I had rung them to ask them to come and pick them up to take care of them before I went into hospital. I came home after the miscarriage to an empty house. Some friends told me I could spend New Year's Eve with them but only if I didn't cry! Great! One week after my miscarriage you can imagine how much crying I wanted to do but I sat there on New Year's Eve and I did as I was told. I kept my feelings to myself and didn't cry. It was very hard! I was devastated about losing my baby and extremely emotional. I couldn't believe how inconsiderate everyone around me was being.

My fiancé had committed the ultimate betrayal in my mind; he should have been there to love and support me and our baby yet he wasn't. He ran as fast as he could to get away from the situation. Once he did that it was all over as far as I was concerned. It was the ultimate deal breaker for me. I had finally seen the light and from this tragic event I was given the wake-up call I so desperately needed. I knew I had to change my behaviour and my attitude once and for all.

Throughout all of this grief, or because of it, it occurred to me ever so slowly that I needed to stop being so self-destructive through my actions. So I stopped looking, stopped searching for something that was so intangible I didn't even know what it was, and I certainly stopped hoping. I stopped living my life through whims and stopped being dictated to by my emotions.

Eventually I recovered from the miscarriage – that is, if you ever really recover from losing a child – and vowed to be celibate for the rest of my life! I told myself I was never going to date again. I was never going through all that pain again. I began the journey of trying to love myself. I was trying to rekindle my relationship with myself because it was important to me to move forward in a positive and constructive way.

I really confronted myself about who I was and how I had been living my life. I had to stop going on this emotional roller coaster ride. I can see now that so much of my behaviour up to that point was about my desperate need to find acceptance, to love someone and to be loved back. I didn't understand the concept of loving and respecting myself first but thought that I could find fulfilment and happiness by just being loved and cherished by another even if I didn't hold myself in much regard. It took me a long time to realise it doesn't work that way.

I was starting to understand that maybe it wasn't everybody else's fault all the time. I had to start taking some responsibility for my own actions.

I didn't realise it at the time but I had actually been attracting these bad relationships. Today I am privileged to work with many women who are what I call broken souls. They are women who have no confidence in themselves or their ability to make their own decisions and be mistress of their own destiny. Some of them are victims of physical and/or verbal abuse; some of them have lived with a very dominant partner with little regard for their autonomy and emotional needs and others are just not confident in finding their own identity, constrained by the roles and expectations society places on them to be good wives and mothers. Through all of my experiences and challenges I was finally given the opportunity to open my eyes and look deep into myself at this stage of my life and begin the process of turning things around. If what they say is true, and we all learn from our experiences both good and bad, then at a very young age I had a load of ammunition to add to my arsenal of knowledge to turn my life into something better.

The children and I moved to Drysdale, on the Bellarine Peninsula, and it was there that things started to turn around. Many years later I still live in Drysdale so I figure that some part of that decision must have been the right one. I was able to get public housing, which was really cheap so that helped me raise the children on what I could earn. I also thought the local school was fantastic for my children. I was determined to give them the best education I could because I hadn't got past form three (year 9) and I wanted so much more for them.

I have always worked and was happy to try my hand at just about anything to earn a decent dollar. I worked at the local pub most of the time in the early days. I must say being a barmaid was my super talent! It's easy. You can work in pubs while your kids are asleep with a babysitter; it seemed to work really well for me. I have also been a medical receptionist, which I loved but I can't stand the sight of blood so that was a bit short-lived.

I never rang home and I never asked for any help. I was determined to not look back but to keep looking forwards and make the best of my life. I had learnt from a very young age to be determined and combined with a little bit of luck and some good management I was able to keep moving on. I didn't buy a book on how to become a housekeeper or a mother, I just slowly learnt through trial and error and a desire to succeed. Sheer guts and determination got me through most days. I'd constantly tell myself 'I'll succeed and if anyone doubts me I'll show them I can do it and do it well!' I was only living three hours away from Rochester but I was determined to not go back there until I had made a success of my life. I didn't want the townsfolk and the friends I had grown up with to pity me or feel any sense of resignation about the decisions I had made in my life.

I eventually got to the stage where I was really comfortable with my journey. I felt peaceful about where I was. I thought that I couldn't be hurt any more and that nobody could deal out anything I wasn't going to be able to cope with. I stopped making stupid decisions and instead I started making good ones. I worked my way through many issues I had been hanging onto. I still keep working on 'me' today; I'm still a work in progress and I don't think I'll ever stop. Nor do I want to. I don't believe it is healthy to stall in our personal growth and development at any stage of our life.

Before the death of my brother, my father had remarried. When I first heard about this I immediately found myself harbouring a deep-seated resentment towards his new wife, my stepmother. I didn't even know her; I had met her but really had no idea who she was or what she was like. I became my mother's ally in my resentment towards my stepmother which, in view of the circumstances under which she came into my father's life, was not entirely unusual. I used my resentment towards my stepmother to avoid trying to sort out my relationship with my father. By adopting this type of mindset I gave myself permission to avoid any form of contact with him. It was a convenient excuse to avoid coming to terms with some of my past..

I held onto that resentment for a very long time but one day, about ten or twelve years ago, my father drove up the drive where we are living now and I went into an absolute panic. A friend of mine was there and was bemused to see the state I was getting myself in and started to laugh. 'What on earth is the matter Sandi?' she asked somewhat incredulously.

'It's my father!'

My friend started laughing at me.

'So? What's the big deal? He's not the grim reaper!'

'You don't understand,' I said. 'I don't know who he is any more or why he is here or how I am meant to behave. What am I meant to say to him?' All of a sudden it became apparent to me that I had no idea who my father was as a man. My only memory of him was as a strict and somewhat intimidating figure from my childhood.

I realised that it was time for me, the grown-up Sandi, to put the past behind me and get to know my father through adult eyes. We went out to dinner that night and I asked David to come with me. 'For heaven's sake,' I said, 'could you please talk to him. This is really awkward, I don't know what to say to him!' I was way out of my depth emotionally.

I knew that over the years my other siblings had slowly rekindled their relationships with our father. I felt there may have been more reticence and maybe a touch of resentment that lingered between my father and I because it had been my actions, after all, that had exposed the cracks in his and Mum's marriage. Silly isn't it? I wasn't the one having the affair, which was the real reason the marriage broke up.

My father has since shared with me his sadness and remorse which came bubbling to the surface with the death of my brother. I think he regretted what had become of our relationship and he was trying to make peace with many things in his life, including his relationship with me. I admire the fact that he was man enough to admit that and because of that I feel I'm the luckiest woman in the world! I have two sets of parents, my father and his second wife and my mother and her second husband. They are all amazing, caring and inspirational people. They all have something different to contribute to their families and we are all enriched by the experience.

When I actually put aside my prejudices and took the time to sit down with my stepmother I found she was a wonderful, kind, caring and funny woman. I really enjoy her company and she is now a very important part of my life. I had no further need to see her as 'the dreaded nasty stepmother'. I'm blessed to have her in my life. For a long time I had lost any relationship with her or my father because I wanted to fester away in my own little world of negativity and resentment rather than let go of the past. My natural tendency to be suspicious and negative towards people was ingrained into me from a very young age as a form of self-protection.

I now have a greater understanding of the decisions my parents made all those years ago and the events that took place leading up to those decisions. My mother is one of the people I admire most. I have watched her go through a marriage break-up and divorce at a time when divorce was unacceptable and taboo. She has watched one of her sons go through cancer, she has buried another son, all of her children have gone through divorces, yet she has come through it all with such grace. Mum always seems to have an answer for everything and if she doesn't have the answer she'll cook! I got a lot of my qualities from my mother (except the cooking). She has certainly created in me the conviction that you have to stand up for what you believe in and do so with understanding and compassion. Ten or fifteen years ago I never wanted to be like her (and never imagined I would be) but I'm really proud to have changed and to be a bit like her now. I use the inspiration of her very special qualities to help me in both my personal and professional life.

Chapter 7

David

I got to a point where for the first time in many years I was no longer running away. I was starting to look ahead. The negativity that had previously filled my thoughts and my world was being replaced by something slightly more positive and this started to open doors.

I finally gave myself permission to go out again. I very rarely went out socially because that was not what mothers did! 'You can't go out, you can't have a life because you've got kids,' I'd tell myself. 'You don't have the time and it's a waste of money.' I have learnt that this is a common mantra for women – putting everyone else's needs ahead of their own and losing their identity in the process.

On the odd occasion I did venture out I felt incredibly guilty but I worked really hard at overcoming those feelings – I was entitled to some 'me' time, after all. On one of my first nights out I accidentally poured a couple of drinks on a very handsome man coming up the stairs. I was going down and I tripped, spilling my drink over him and he also spilled his drink over me in the commotion. This was the first time I clapped eyes on the man who would become my darling husband David. I wasn't looking for a new relationship – I was just out to have some fun with my friends, have a break from the children and enjoy a bit of adult company. By this stage I had realised I needed to be less tough on myself, to lighten up a bit and give myself a break. I had worked hard and was raising my children the best way I knew how. I was happy with my independence and being answerable only to myself. There were quite a few parts of me I was starting to appreciate and like. I was on a journey of self-discovery and was re-establishing myself and the fragments of my psyche that I had allowed to be taken away through the ups and downs of my tumultuous young life.

When I first met David it was not love at first sight. I didn't believe in that romantic nonsense after everything I had been through. To me, love was just a whole lot of empty promises and a swag load of disappointment to boot. At the time I had a nonchalant attitude; I had accepted who I was, where I had been and where I was going and as far as I was concerned nothing and no-one else mattered apart from me and my children. David, however, had other ideas and through his quiet persistence and positive attitude he eventually got under my skin and broke down my barriers. He showed me a side to men I hadn't seen before. He showed me there are some men who are good, who have no ulterior motive and do not sit in judgement of others. They just accept you for who you are, warts and all.

After our meeting on the stairs David came around the next day with an excuse to return some money to another friend who had been with us. I invited him in and he hinted at the fact that he would like to see me again and maybe take me out to dinner. 'Hang on a minute mister,' I said. 'You might want to rethink that – I am a single mother with three children. I don't know that I can do that.' His reply set me back on my haunches. 'Oh, where are they? I'd like to meet them.' That certainly was not what I was expecting. David was a natural with my children and seemed to revel in taking on a parenting role of his own volition. Here was this young man, three years younger than me, who had no children of his own, no attachments and no commitments. But the moment he met my kids he simply stepped into being the male role model in their lives.

David had an enormous influence on me at a crucial time in my life when I was putting distance between the angry and destructive me and working towards being a more responsible, open-minded young woman. He accepted me for who I was and he came without an agenda. Pretty soon after our second date he seemed to want to throw himself into our lives in a hands-on way. Never one to stand back when there was a job to be done, he rendered me speechless when one day he asked me to show him how to change a nappy! He slipped effortlessly into a co-parenting role. He did his bit, I did mine. Neither he nor I ever discussed what our various roles would be, it all just happened.

One day David said to me, 'We are in this together, you and me. I want to be their father.' I was delighted and said, 'I don't have a problem with that at all!' However I wasn't really interested in going full bore at this relationship. I decided that if he stuck around and continued to behave the way he had been, maybe he would convince me that this relationship might work. His persistence paid off and we have been married for over twenty years now.

David won me over with his integrity, honour, accountability, persistence and humility. He brought all of these qualities into our relationship. I had never experienced any of these before. I'd seen glimpses of them in some people but not all the time and he showed them to me continuously. He was rodeoing back then and he had a real drive, a passion and a competitiveness about him that would not let anything stand in his way. I knew I had the same attributes and this made us a good pair. We were thoroughly compatible; I understood him really, really well.

David accepted me just as I was, there were no rules. Well, actually there was one rule. 'If I am going to be with you,' he told me, 'these children are mine too and it's not negotiable. That means I change their nappies, I feed them, I go to sporting events, I am their father in every sense of the word.' He understood that they might want to see their biological fathers but in the home environment he was their father and that was that. My children were an integral part of me and in his mind it was simple: he loved me and so he loved my children. Over the years I have seen many single mothers try to establish a new relationship with a man who has no regard for the fact that they are a mother and sometimes are openly hostile towards their children because they take the attention away from him. Some don't want be involved with the children at all. In my eyes these women deserve a man who will not only love them but will love their kids and they should settle for nothing less. Sadly, many women are so overwhelmed by taking full responsibility for raising their children that they will jump into any relationship regardless of the consequences. I tried doing that: I tried being with men who said they loved me but didn't want my children and it doesn't work. I was only deceiving myself and denying my children something that they should have had. I know now that my children deserve to be an integral part of a loving relationship, not just excess baggage. All children deserve that.

My oldest son probably had the hardest time adapting to David. At age four or five he had been the 'man' of the house, a role he had to give up when David arrived. He rebelled for a little while but it wasn't long before he settled back into the joy of just being a little boy. My youngest child was too young to remember a man in his life and he just lapped up being loved by David!

We developed a wonderful circle of new friends around us in no time at all. They were 'our' friends, not mine and not his specifically. They are still among our closest friends today and we really enjoy spending time with one another.

One of the most significant moments in my life at that time was when David took me to meet his mother and father. You can imagine how I felt; I was terrified, waiting for a negative response or the hint of disapproval about their darling son being involved with a woman with three children. I braced myself for what I thought would be their reaction and then subsequently the possibility that David might see me through their eyes and leave. I had been waiting for the day he would go and I figured that this would be the catalyst. When I walked into his parents' house I found them to be the most humble, giving, warm-hearted and beautiful people. His mother grabbed me and hugged me and said, 'So you're the one that's won my baby's heart! Good for you!' She sat the kids on her lap and told me that any time we wanted to go out she would babysit. I never felt anything but love and acceptance from them towards me and my children and they allowed my children to be a part of their family from the very first moment they met them. If their son loved me, that was good enough for them.

David's parents taught me so much by opening up their hearts and their home and allowing me to be part of their family with all their celebrations and traditions. The most regular of these was Sunday lunch and we were all expected to be part of this. For me that was just the most amazing feeling and I loved it. When David and I first started going out, his parents or a girlfriend of mine would babysit for us on a Saturday night. We'd be a bit hazy the next day and turn up for lunch looking a little worse for wear; they'd just laugh at us and make fun of us. It was all healthy stuff. God bless them for being such wonderful, genuine people. There are some amazing people in this world and David's parents were without a doubt well up amongst them. No wonder they were able to raise such a wonderful son! I still consider his parents two of the most amazing people I have had the privilege of meeting. Sadly, both of David's parents are no longer with us but I shall always be grateful to them. We miss them terribly.

From the very beginning our relationship was established by just being ourselves with one another. We never analysed anything or asked each other what we were doing or where we were going within our relationship. We created the greatest team from the beginning. We were equals – it was such a natural thing to be. He didn't do some of things I'd experienced before, such as disappearing to the pub on a Friday night, because I had the kids. When we did something we did it together and made a family affair of it. We had a ton of fun, to the point where every weekend we'd have half a dozen people calling in because our house was so much fun. The kids were loved by everyone. It was a healthy relationship and our friends were good, kind-hearted people. The friends we made together were good for us and they loved us for who we were.

It seemed only natural for us to become engaged and then married. I came home one day with an engagement ring and said, 'Whaddaya reckon?' and David said, 'Righto!' He put the ring on my finger and then said, 'Quick, let's go tell Mum!' It wasn't all that romantic but it seemed the most natural thing in the world for us to do. We planned on getting married at some stage but it took forever to actually happen as we were too busy living our lives and having fun. David was rodeoing here and there, which saw us travelling around the country. We enjoyed spending time together as a family, doing all sorts of things wherever we were. This was when I knew I was really starting to live a good life and I was 'normal'.

We only ended up getting married because one of our kids entered us in a wedding competition and we won. One day a guy rang me and said that we'd won our wedding through a competition. I didn't remember entering the competition and thought it was our insurance agent with whom we had a great relationship playing a joke on us. I said, 'Oh John, you're pulling my leg!' and promptly hung up on him. Two minutes later the phone rang again and the guy very nicely asked me to listen as he had something he wanted to explain. We had won a competition. I asked him what it was and he said a wedding. We won the whole lot – the only thing we had to pay for was the reception.

Our wedding was absolutely amazing. Practically my entire family made the effort to attend. My sister was my bridesmaid and my brother gave me away instead of my father. I hadn't seen Dad more than a handful of times over the previous ten years, none of which had been happy times, which is why I asked my brother to do me the honour of giving me away.

David and I have created a wonderful life together. I wouldn't change a thing but in the early stages of our relationship, when it became apparent to me that this was a genuine long-term relationship, I went into self-protection mode. On one hand I was more than ready to emotionally invest in the relationship but on the other I had to make sure I wasn't going to get hurt again. I would put him to the test all the time. I'd say, 'If you're going to leave me, leave me now!' I would push, push, push to get him to prove his love and I would then prepare myself for him leaving because that was all I had ever known. 'You're promising me all this stuff but I don't believe you, you're going to leave me, I just know it – so go on, go now!' I became intolerable and an emotional control freak to the nth degree. David, being the passive, laid-back man that he is, allowed me to go on that journey. He didn't like it but he tolerated it because his love for me was so strong.

So when I found out I was pregnant with our son I went into emotional overdrive. I could see everything unravelling again as it had with the other men in my life. I got myself into such a fearful, illogical dither before I plucked up the courage to tell David. We had discussed having children. I had told him that if I had not met him I would never have considered having more children, but that I would do it because he would be the most wonderful father and was worthy of having children of his own. He was already a wonderful parent to three who weren't his, claiming that they were his children and still to this day he says they are his children and nobody else's. I felt that he should be given the opportunity and gift of fathering his own children.

I didn't expect the pregnancy to open up the emotional can of worms it did for me. It didn't matter how much work I had done to feel secure within the relationship, I started thinking, 'You've done it again! Three strikes and you're out, girl, and this is your fourth.' The sad part was that if things went the way I was fearing they might, it was my three children who would ultimately suffer the most because they loved David so very much. Before he came along my children hadn't formed an attachment to anyone because I hadn't allowed them to or they had been too young.

I prepared myself for what I thought was to come. I sat David down and said, 'By the way, what we had planned on doing in a year's time we've done now and I'm pregnant.' And from the smile on his face, the look of contentment, without a word from his mouth I knew that it wasn't going to be the same as it had been before. The satisfaction that he showed and the emotion on his face, knowing he was going to be a father, was beautiful and from that moment I knew we were going to be okay. David's calm, consistent strength and love showed me that I didn't need to fear he would abandon me and so I stopped doubting him and stopped doubting our relationship. My days of emotional self-destruction were finally coming to an end. Through David's encouragement and support I was eventually able to re-establish a relationship with my family. They came to our wedding and from that day we started to see one another again and be supportive of one another. My friendships became stronger and more meaningful and I finally started to pick the right people to be in my life.

David and I eventually had two boys and for the first time I found out what it was really meant to be like when you are pregnant and sharing the birth of your children with their father. The difference it made having the love and support of a husband and family was amazing and extremely comforting. I was enveloped in a shroud of love and security and felt that finally I had found the peace I had been searching for.

I feel that the two sons we had together have completed David. He is one of the most wonderful fathers I have ever met. His children, all of them, are his best friends. His manner and sense of peace and serenity combined with his sense of humour and fun are some of the many things they all love about him. Calm and consistent, that is David. He was and is that for me and for the kids.

With the arrival of our sons and the development of our family, David and the boys inadvertently taught me something about my previous life and relationships. This was pretty confronting because I began to realise how unfairly I had been treated by others. I spent a lot of time thinking about this, examining all aspects and trying to figure out why and how it had happened. The more I was able to explore within the security of my marriage and family the more I began to understand and I felt acceptance developing without bitterness or remorse for what had occurred. With that acceptance and understanding I discovered a totally new emotion for me – compassion. No longer did I have my defences up. I ceased to be suspicious and dismissive of people around me for fear of being used and hurt. I started to see and look for the good in people, not the bad. I knew that my nickname around town was 'the bitch' because of my attitude and hostility towards others. I had never taken the time to try to understand someone else's perspective. I had no compassion until then. It was quite a revelation in more ways than one.

Chapter 8

My new family

David has never changed. Over time he has been able to influence my reactions in a positive way. I think he learnt to behave like this as a child; in fact, he was probably born that way. He's is a calm, fun-loving person who does not get overly emotional over trivial events. He loves living his life to the best of his ability and does not get involved in too much drama. He's one of the few people I know who loves his own company. He enjoys being around people but he also loves being on his own. We share a lot of deep and powerful moments – some of the most powerful are when we are sitting in the car saying nothing to one another at all. There is no need, there is the comfort of not needing to say anything at all.

It was such a turnaround to go from a destructive lifestyle like mine into this kind of relationship. I had to learn new ways to behave and react. In the beginning I used to get furious with him. It was as if I wanted him to be miserable with me. But that was just not the way he was born. True to his manner he ever so slowly showed me how much of a control freak I was. It is so tiring controlling everyone and everything around you in an attempt to protect yourself from hurt and disappointment. He quietly brought this to my attention and in my inimitable way I was quite loud in dealing with it!

Everyone had to do what I told them and no-one could ever do it as well as me. 'Don't bother vacuuming, I'll do it!' I'd say. Or they'd make their bed and I'd go in and tell them they hadn't done it right. Martyr syndrome and control freak all wrapped up in one. It was all about me protecting myself from being hurt, but I didn't know that at the time. I just thought that if I had everyone under control I was safe.

But I wasn't safe. I was making a very unsafe place for myself and everyone else. I'd walk into the room to watch TV at night and when I'd sit down all of a sudden five children and my husband left. They wanted to get out of my way before I got on their case. With the attitude I had at the time I would think, 'It's all right, none of you wanted to watch what I wanted to watch anyway, so just go away, the lot of you!' And I would nag David: 'You've got to do this, you've got to do that,' and I'd always be snapping at him unfairly because I didn't know what else to do.

I see many women who try to control everything around them and they do so out of fear – fear of being hurt, criticised or ridiculed, fear of being made to feel inferior and fear of not being 'in control'. We think that we can control what we fear but in doing so we focus so much on that fear that we tend to attract the very thing we are afraid of. I had done that most of my life and I did it to David. I thought that if I pushed enough to force him to leave he would, and then I could stand back and justify my actions by telling myself 'See, I knew it!' What a whole lot of self-fulfilling self-sabotage at its very finest!

David, however, slowly peeled back my protective layers. He wasn't even aware he was doing it. He loved me so unconditionally that when he did give me some constructive criticism I would, for the first time in my life, listen and take it on board. He wasn't judgemental and he supported and loved me warts and all.

But about four or five years into our relationship he finally got sick and tired of my antics and my controlling ways and made me stop and take a good long look at myself. One day he quietly said, 'We love you, we don't want to live without you but you're no fun to be around.' He was right and it was just what I needed to hear. I sat down and had a good long talk (or more like a tussle and a scream) with myself. How could I be so awful and make those I loved the most so miserable? I was my own worst enemy and I wasn't being fair to anyone let alone myself. This epiphany came just as we were trying to get our business off the ground and make David's training and work with horses a success. I was focused on 'making' him a success instead of letting him become successful. David quietly made me look at how things were and what I was doing but he also allowed me the time and freedom to fix it. His support is unconditional without the 'rules and regulations' so often attached and unsaid in a relationship. If I said I wanted to go away for a girls' weekend because I just wanted to go thrash things out around the table with girlfriends, or if I wanted to go away and be alone, he always gave me the freedom to do so. In doing that he allowed me to make my own mistakes and discover who I was.

After I realised what I had been inadvertently doing to the people I loved I went on a guilt trip. At times the pendulum swung the other way and I found myself becoming a bit of a pushover in order not to hurt anyone any more. The rules of the game changed – behaviour I previously hadn't condoned or tolerated became acceptable. I swung from being very black and white with how I saw my interaction with the world to finding out that there were indeed many shades of grey. It was when I found those shades of grey that I started to develop empathy and understanding. Prior to this people only ever had one chance with me and if they hurt me once, that was it and they were out of my life for good.

David has never been concerned about the fact that I was a teenage mother or about how I grew up and the mistakes I made. He's always said to me, 'You are who you are, that's all I care about.' He's never asked me a single question about my life before I met him. He has never made me feel guilty or insecure about anything about myself. He probably won't even read this book! Of course he's heard me talk about it to the kids and to other people, but to him my past is of no concern to him and doesn't define our relationship. He simply made me accountable to myself and required that I step up and be the best I could be. I feel I have done the same for him too. He has certainly given me the security to be myself and has allowed me to go on a journey of discovery to truly find myself without any judgement or criticism. Even today he won't challenge me on my own journey, he just lets me be and then when I make a mistake he picks me up and dusts me off and we keep going. He's never derogatory and has never put me down. In my eyes he's everything to me. I would not tolerate a bad word said about him and I know he would do the same for me. We always have each other's back.

Many things helped me to see life differently and to change my behaviour but at the core of it was my relationship with David. Meeting new people, sharing my story and hearing their own stories helped too. I stopped seeing myself as the only person who'd ever experienced bad things and I started seeing that others had been through tough times too and this humbled me. I had survived my traumas and difficult, dark times but there were many women who hadn't. When I had been completely on my own, I thought I was the only one in the world going through hell. It was through being able to thrash it out in my own head or with friends and family, and then having a soft place to fall, that I realised I was actually okay.

The first ten years of my relationship with David enabled me to start to understand myself and also learn to understand others. I was able to stand back and look at the things I had done, as well as what had been done to me. I believe I developed some wisdom and learnt to see things in people that I hadn't previously. However, I didn't let my experiences become meaningless to me. There had to be a reason for them and there had to be a meaning that would become apparent. Through this journey of discovery there was a realisation and an awakening within me. I started to experience emotions that were previously quite foreign to me – empathy, compassion and, the most significant of all, forgiveness.

Chapter 9

Forgiveness

There are times when I reflect upon my life and realise I have become the person I am today because of all that has gone before. It is the same for all of us. My understanding of people and their behaviour and how people can suffer so much in their lives is something I can sense now because I think I've been through and experienced every emotion a woman can feel. Sometimes we have to accept that we cannot own or be responsible for everything that happened to us as children, simply because we were just that: children. I have met many women who have been victims of similar experiences as my own. The repercussions are devastating to their spiritual and emotional health. It infiltrates their life in the most insidious ways.

Very often I understand the reactions people have and the way they behave because of my own experiences. We all react to things that happen to us in many unusual and challenging ways but often we don't understand why. We find out that we have triggers. These triggers can seem meaningless and trivial to others but we may react in such an out of control or illogical way that we and others around us don't actually understand what is going on.

I believe I have always had an open heart. Sometimes it got bashed around, became a little tarnished and bruised, but I never really shut it down for good. This has been my greatest burden at times but also, I now realise, my greatest gift as even in the darkest hours it enabled me to still feel a tiny glimmer of hope, a strong sense of survival and the drive to keep learning and improving my circumstances no matter what life threw up at me.

When eventually I stopped fighting everyone and everything around me I was able to let go of the anger and ask myself 'What are you fighting for?' I separated my actions and emotions. I learnt not to be so reactive to things. I started listening more, and the more I listened the more I learnt.

One day I was watching *Dr Phil*. I heard him say, 'Forgiveness is something you give yourself'. It was the wake-up call I needed. What an epiphany. The penny finally dropped. Let go of the anger. This new attitude began to overflow into everything in my life. I could feel the changes within me. I got so excited. I wanted to learn more and went off exploring to find out as much information as I could. The more interested I became in myself the more I was able to stand back and analyse where I was and what had brought me to that point. I realised that what I said and what I felt were two entirely different things – at that point I had no idea how to give my authentic self her voice.

I believed that forgiveness was something you gave to someone for something they had done to you. It was only when I heard Dr Phil say it was something you also gave yourself that I understood I was ready to heal some very old wounds. I was ready to find forgiveness within myself towards those whom I felt had hurt me and so had deliberately shut out of my life.

The first person that I needed to apply this to was my father. I had built up an impenetrable mantel around myself in relation to my feelings towards him. I tried to make sure that nothing he did or said could get in and affect me. I didn't want anything from him and I made sure I took nothing away emotionally from him on the odd occasion we met. I probably appeared to be quite uncaring and offhand towards him. The more I thought about it the more I realised how absolutely grief stricken I was about how I thought he had abandonned me and how much it had affected my life. When I gave myself permission to find forgiveness within, I started to heal and doors opened up for me emotionally.

Initially it was my father who extended the olive branch, when he arrived that day unannounced at our home. I remember very early in our 'new relationship' going out to dinner with him and Nana May, his wife. I sat beside Nana May and during the course of the evening I learnt that she was a very funny, kind, good-natured woman with a heart of gold. David got on with her too and said how lovely she was. I loved and respected him and his opinions and so through fresh eyes I began to understand that I had never really allowed myself to get to know Nana May until then. She was 'the other woman', the one who had stolen my father away from me and broken my mother's heart in the process.

I made a choice to forgive my father. I was sick of the walls I had built up to protect myself from being hurt or taken advantage of. I decided that what I had to do was show him 'me', to show him who I am. I let him into my world, talked about my work, my family and my dreams and aspirations. I allowed him to get to know me and what I stand for. Over time his pride in me developed. This means the world to me. I have come to understand that out of all of his children I am the one most like him.

My father and I haven't really sat down and had a 'heart to heart' about what transpired all those years ago. I know he feels very vulnerable and guilty about what he did. He will occasionally bring it up, and I think it is far more appropriate that he is the one to do so. I don't need to keep metaphorically beating him around the head about it. I have found peace and understanding within myself. If he does want to talk about it, I just sit and listen. It is not for me to pass judgement on his actions. In hindsight, perhaps he could have gone about things differently; how many of us would have done something differently in our lives with the wisdom of hindsight? My father carries enough grief and guilt over the things he could have done better or differently during his life, he doesn't need anyone else to put that on him as well. I wish he could find some peace. I think the relationship we have today has gone some way in helping him find that little bit of peace.

Dad and Nana May live on our property now and I love having them here. They are such an integral part of our family. It is a joy to see them revelling in their roles as grandparents to our sons. I love seeing Dad tootle around the garden always fixing things, doing things and enjoying time with David, who he sees more as a son than a son-in-law. I often come inside and find that darling Nana May has restocked the fridge with home-baked goodies or done the pile of dishes or ironing that I was girding my loins to do. I feel blessed to have their quiet, steady presence in our lives.

We can all choose to forgive those around us. It is probably one of the most important qualities to possess and understand, and has to be given in the right manner. True forgiveness lays a lot of things to rest but I believe you have to earn forgiveness in your own mind. My father earnt my forgiveness by coming back into my life. He also allowed me to be me, to show him who I was without judgement or criticism. He was just there, which he hadn't been for such a very long time. He earnt my trust and my respect as his appearance back in my life enabled me to find forgiveness. I am so very grateful for that.

Many of the women I meet need to learn how to forgive in this manner. They say they have forgiven this or that, forgiven someone who has done something to them but I can see that they haven't because they haven't given themselves that gift of forgiveness. I can see it in their eyes – I can see their pain still. It is a choice we can give ourselves. Yes, it is really that simple: we can make a choice and by choosing to forgive we find clarity and eventually peace and acceptance.

Through forgiveness we can take ownership of our past no matter what has happened to us previously – no matter what the injustice or hurt that has been inflicted upon us either by ourselves or others. We can lay the past to rest and move forward with our lives in the most positive way imaginable.

Through forgiveness I now live my life with the true conviction and knowledge of who I am. I am no longer a victim, I am no longer filled with bitterness and anger. I am not particularly fussed whether someone likes me or not but I am passionate about being understood. I believe that we all deserve to live life to the best of our abilities and get the very best from ourselves. I am no longer interested in being critical of how others conduct themselves in their lives and I will not stand in judgement of them.

Chapter 10

Compassion

I will tell you who I am and say what I mean. If I am going to have a conversation with anyone it will always be a truthful one. If it is not then I won't have it. I will not go back to the way I lived the first part of my life; I will not go back to lies, cover-ups and silent omissions to suit someone else's expectations or to make sure no-one gets hurt or offended.

I want to give hope to the women I work with because I wished someone, just one person, had come to me and asked, 'Are you okay?' when I was alone and abandoned all those years ago. I put the 'circle' or round-table discussion at the start of each day at every clinic and camp I conduct because I believe every woman has the right to be heard, the right to be understood, the right to tell their story in a safe place with kindred spirits who will not sit in judgement or be critical. I know what it is like to be criticised, judged and tormented, and the burden of it is at times overwhelming – it is almost always destructive. Within the safety of the circle all the participants listen to one another with compassion. I truly believe that it gives those women who are prepared to share a little of themselves some peace, and whatever their fear is it is taken away within that safe, nurturing environment. They see that they can allow themselves to feel whatever it is they are feeling at that particular moment, for a brief time in their life, for all of their life – there is no time limit or restriction on their feelings. They give themselves permission to be present and honest in that circle as I am with them. It can sometimes be confronting because emotions that might have lain hidden for a long time come bubbling to the surface; but most of all, the circle and the love, support and compassion shown are liberating and empowering.

Compassion is something we all need to find within ourselves. It took me a long time to find it let alone understand it. To me, compassion is having an understanding of what someone else is going through and with that understanding there is a oneness, a kindred feeling as you accept their hurt for what it is. Compassion often carries with it a touch of sadness, a softness and depth of emotion and understanding for what is being unveiled before you by another as they allow you into their innermost emotional world; they will allow you to share with them their vulnerabilities, their weaknesses, their faults and their flaws.

Compassion is about seeing behind someone's words or actions. To me, compassion is when you sit in the moment with someone and their emotions and allow it to be as it is with an understanding and a stillness of mind and soul. There is an all pervading sense of the 'now', and peace.

I had little compassion in my younger years. I doubt I really understood what it meant. It wasn't until I was a woman in my thirties that I discovered compassion. My mother and I had a distant relationship for many years. I think it was because I wasn't at all interested in revisiting my past in any way, shape or form. I saw going back as a negative. I was uneasy, and thought that if I did go back and face some of my past a floodgate of emotion would open up that I knew I would not be able to cope with. It was many years before I was emotionally stable or mature enough to do so. The relationship with my mother stagnated for a while and so we were a little distant with one another.

When I eventually decided I needed to find peace in my life I did revisit my past and in so doing my mother became my greatest teacher, bless her. I began to think about her as a woman. I know that sounds a funny thing to say – she was after all just that, a woman. But what I mean is I learnt to look at my mother woman to woman, not child to mother. It was when I was able to do this that I saw her and her amazing strength and dignity with all she had been through. I saw a woman whose whole life had been turned upside down when her husband left her for another woman, who then had to deal with her fourteen-year-old daughter being pregnant and having a baby and then on top of all of this buried her son. Amidst all this chaos and grief my mother had to redefine herself and push herself to do things she hadn't done before, such as learning how to drive and getting her licence. Her world as a wife and mother had imploded and she was left alone and heartbroken.

When I reflected upon this I started to feel true compassion for her and for all she had been through. I cannot imagine the pain of burying one of your adult children – I pray that I never find out. How do you ever get over that? How do you even get up the next day, and the next and the next? When my brother died it didn't even occur to me how it was affecting my mother. I was grieving for the loss of my brother; my focus was on my loss, not on anyone else's.

My mother stayed on in Rochester and still lives there today. She is very much loved and respected in the town and is known to all as Nanny Yvonne. She has been on just about every community committee ever formed in Rochester and she works tirelessly for the town and its citizens. Her warmth and generosity is known by many and she is the one who will organise Christmas in July functions in her house for the elderly and the lonely. She has always been a very giving soul and you never walk out of her house without having been very well fed (she is a great cook of good old-fashioned wholesome food) and probably carrying a cake, casserole or batch of biscuits under your arm to set you on your way. This is typical of her generation and that good old Australian work ethic – they had little but they worked hard, were generous, warm and friendly and always looked out for others. What a pity this seems to be a dying trait along with their generation. We can learn much from their humility and humanity.

My mother was the softie in the family and hated confrontation, trouble or any sort of bad vibes. When my father left she toughened up a bit and developed the tenacity and resilience she needed to get on with her life. Growing up I never felt any negativity or had any beef with my mother. There was never a bad word spoken between us until my father left and my world was turned upside down, and then we both began to behave very differently but that was my issue not hers. I didn't have the maturity to know how to cope any differently so I rebelled and became very bitter and resentful, and a wedge formed in our relationship because of it. It is easier to blame someone else than to take a good, hard look at yourself when things are not to your liking!

At the time when I needed a role model as a little girl, my mother was in crisis. No-one ever taught me how to cook, how to look after a house, do housework, budget, pay bills or shop. I had to learn all of this through trial and error. (I must admit I have never learnt the cooking thing – I am very good at eating, but cooking? Nah – not my thing!) While I was learning all of this and making plenty of mistakes, I had an overwhelming feeling that I was watching my real life, or what should have been my real life, going on outside the window while I was stuck inside up to my eyeballs in domesticity.

And so through all of my attempts to grow and find peace I had to understand my various levels of dysfunction otherwise I was going to be stuck where I was forever. Bit by bit I looked at one emotion at a time, which was the only way I could find the answers and the key that would open up my heart without destroying me. If I had let the negative self-chatter rear its ugly head again I knew it wouldn't work. I made a conscious effort to see myself and what I had done and who I truly was through my own eyes and not through someone else's.

By discovering my true self, by finding my own autonomy I was finally able to look at things through fresh eyes. The child raising the children became a woman raising her children and even though my two eldest children had seen me at my lowest ebb – warts and all – we hung in there together and I believe I have given them a great message about keeping on keeping on, working hard, never giving up and never giving in. I see them conducting their lives with this work ethic and morality as young adults today and I am so proud of them.

Over the years I have developed my own set of laws and rules and I use these as a way of defining myself. They incorporate love, loyalty, trust, honesty, integrity, humour and resilience. I have used all of these attributes throughout my life in varying degrees and when some were missing, such as trust and love, I would compensate for their absence with honesty and resilience. Using my system I work on whatever pops up – it doesn't matter what it is. For example, if a question of honesty (mine or another's) pops up I ask myself, 'Is it real?' To answer this question I need to be present in the moment and have a full understanding of what it is that is presenting itself to me. I use this time and time again in my life, both at a personal level and a professional level. It is so very important to really listen to what people are telling you. If they are paying you the compliment of telling you something about themselves or sharing something with you then it is only right that you pay them the courtesy of listening and being present in the moment with their thoughts and conversation. I know many people who just nod and smile and I watch their eyes glaze over and their concentration drift when they are being spoken to – it is actually quite rude. Don't they realise that most people are onto them in this regard? This makes the person who is talking clam up and they will withdraw into themselves. Some people who have never really opened up about themselves and their feelings can be extremely shy and cautious, and one little hint that you are not listening or want to put in your two bob's worth about yourself will send them flying back into their shell of self-protection and the moment is lost.

If I hadn't learnt how to listen I wouldn't have learnt about compassion. Listening helps create your own inner voice and dialogue. It is a very powerful tool. I always make sure I am listening and not just hearing. If I feel myself drifting I immediately correct myself and refocus.

Chapter 11

Empathy

Empathy and compassion are very similar and can go hand in hand, although at times they are, and need to be, quite separate. Empathy is, I believe, when you take the next step by acknowledging what has transpired with a sense of hope, and an attitude of 'Okay let's get on with it! We can do something with this – let's move forward! What can we learn, what opportunities does this present to us?' For me, empathy is about having a plan and figuring out what steps are needed to put that plan into practice.

One of my dearest friends, Annie, devastatingly lost everything in Victoria's Black Saturday bushfires in 2009: her home, her business, her husband's business. Everything was gone. Her family was lucky to escape with their lives. For two days after I got the news my heart was oozing compassion; I felt gutted for her and I was grieving for all that she had lost. It was a time to just sit in the sadness and enormity of the moment. But then my empathy kicked in and I thought to myself 'Okay, what can I do about this? What plans need to be put in place to deal with this horrible situation?' This is how I see empathy and this is how it works for me.

On the third day I knew what I had to do, so I set to work to help find a home for Annie and her family. She knew she was more than welcome to stay with us for as long as needed but it was really important to her that her family stay within their community where they could start helping their friends and neighbours to clean up, sift through the chaos and ever so slowly start to rebuild their lives. I suppose there was a sense of security being with people who had some idea how you may be feeling, as they were living it too. Those of us who have been fortunate to never experience such a thing can only imagine what it might be like. We can be filled with compassion and sympathy but we cannot really understand unless we have lived it ourselves.

Not only was a new home sourced but I put out an SOS to all our friends and family and within twenty-four hours we had donations of food, household items, tools, money, hay and feed for her horses – you name it, we were given it. People were amazingly generous and in true Aussie fashion dug deep to help someone in need. Some of the contributors didn't even know Annie but that mattered little, they all wanted to help and be a part of it.

When it was safe to travel into the bushfire area, a few friends accompanied me to Annie's new 'home' with trailer loads of goods. Some items were doubled up on, trebled up on and even quadrupled up on – I think at one stage they had three or four lawn mowers! This didn't matter because it simply meant any extras could be given to someone else in need.

For many weeks I went backwards and forwards helping Annie. As you can imagine, she needed a lot of help emotionally and I sat with her many a time while she cried, got angry, got complacent and sometimes bitter and then resentful – all stages of the grieving process. It was a gruelling time for her and her family but she has come through it, has created a new life for herself and is really kicking some goals. I am proud of her and I was so pleased I was able to help her get back on track in some small way. I see her as a trailblazer as she recreates herself and forms a new and invigorating life around her after such sorrow, loss and tragedy.

The emotions of compassion and empathy often come into play when we are dealing with such grief and sorrow. I believe that you can understand a lot of what people are going through if you have a true depth of understanding about what loss, grief, hurt, abandonment and sadness feel like. I had never lost everything in a bushfire and I hope I am never in that position but I do know about loss, I do know about grief, hurt, abandonment and sadness. I was able to help Annie through the emotions with compassion and empathy. I believe all those who have experienced these emotions are able to help others with compassion and empathy.

I love when I see moments of sheer and utter joy spread over the faces of friends like Annie or the women who have shared fears and emotions at my clinics and camps. I feel such a sense of pride and satisfaction for them and I become engaged in the moment with them and thoroughly enjoy their 'joyfulness'.

Chapter 12

Self-worth and self-esteem

Self-worth and self-belief are the motors for how we think and how we run our lives. If your self-worth is fractured, a by-product is created. To explain, I'll use the analogy of a rearing horse. If you have had a nasty fall from a rearing horse, no matter how competent a rider you may be your confidence in your ability will be fractured or undermined. Even though you may keep riding, it is only natural to be anxious if what you felt just prior to your accident you experience again. The by-product of this is that you may in fact cause the horse to rear again! This of course reinforces your lack of confidence and reinforces your fear of being put in a position where a horse might rear on you. It becomes a vicious cycle that is very hard to break.

If in life you cannot break the cycle of self-doubt and low self-esteem it is very easy to give up on yourself. If you give up on yourself you give up on living the best life you can and, sadly, the end of this fractured state of mind is giving up on life altogether.

There have been many times in my life where I had only a remnant of self-worth floating around somewhere inside me but I refused to give up. I also had a tiny amount of courage that would make me soldier on, and between the two emotions I was able to bounce one off the other and eventually peel back all of my layers and start moving forward, little by little, tiny step by tiny step.

Self-esteem and self-worth are the fertiliser and water that we need to determine our emotional growth. I feel wholly responsible for keeping a handle on this in my own life and to keep working on it, nurturing it and discovering all that I can to continue getting the best out of myself and living the best life I can. It will never be over – it is not a static thing. We are forever evolving and learning and growing, no matter how young or old we are. It is quite complex keeping in balance our emotional, spiritual and physical wellbeing. All three need to be worked on constantly. Sometimes your physical health will need more attention because you are ill, sometimes it will be your emotional health because you are upset or worried and sometimes you just need to stop and focus on your spiritual wellbeing by whatever means you can. If one is totally out of balance for any period of time then rest assured it will throw the other two out as well, so we need to constantly be aware of how we are feeling on all three levels.

For many people it is quite an uncomfortable concept to accept praise or compliments from others. You can see them look a little self-conscious and shy. If you ask someone to tell you something negative about themselves, in a heartbeat they will! Conversely, if you ask the same person to tell you something positive about themselves they will struggle to do so. Bizarre isn't it? Is it because they feel bigheaded and boastful if they say something good about themselves? This is a negative thing that I think is prevalent in all levels of society. Look at what is known in Australia as the tall poppy syndrome. If anyone is seen to be too successful, too rich or too beautiful, people are very quick to criticise them and try to bring them down a peg or two. Why can't we just be happy for them and admire them for what they have achieved?

Similarly, there is this overwhelming idea in the equestrian community that you can very quickly ruin a horse through bad training but it takes a lot longer to train a horse positively. In fact, training is training and takes exactly the same amount of time, whether it be to train positively or negatively – one does not take any longer than the other.

I adopted this sort of methodology myself, as do many others. In my head I would hear all the negative talk and negative labelling which others placed upon me: 'You're bad', 'You didn't do that right', 'You aren't a good mother'. I was so eager to accept the negative and was so resistant to seeing anything good or positive. There is a well known sociological theory called labelling theory. Basically it goes like this: if we are told something often enough – such as 'You're hopeless, you're lazy and you'll never amount to much' even though initially it might not be true – you will start believing the labels people put on you, therefore perpetuating their views about who you are and reinforcing these traits in yourself. Wouldn't we all be better off if we focused on the positive in people and encouraged them to be the best they can and try to help them along the way? Of course we would! However, when we do start to find the positive things within ourselves and start to work on our self-esteem and self-worth, we more often than not feel guilty about it! To live in negativity and with self-doubt and self-loathing is very draining and can be very destructive.

As women, we are often the last ones to give ourselves permission to have what we need to attain self-worth and physical, emotional and spiritual wellbeing. How many women do you know who put their family's needs before their own? I'm guessing the number is more than those who put their own needs first! It can even be as simple as having the overcooked piece of the lamb roast so everyone else has the good bits. So typical of women – always giving, always putting others first. There comes a point, though, when this selflessness can be quite destructive. The mum in the family, the wife in the marriage or the woman in the workplace can become deeply unhappy, feel taken for granted and not heard; there is no surer way to erode any sense of self-worth. So many of the women who come to my clinics and camps are a living testimony to this phenomenon. They try to find some 'me' time and so they want to ride but they always put it off because other things – family needs or their relationships – get in the way. If they do find the time they feel guilty about it and are preoccupied with what they 'should' be doing and so do not enjoy the 'me' time they so desperately need. When they finally manage to come to a clinic or camp, their self-esteem is in their boots along with their confidence in themselves. They feel incompetent, out of their depth emotionally, physically and spiritually. The very fact that they are at a confidence clinic or camp is really positive because they are raising the white flag – they are recognising that they need help and they are prepared to go out and seek that help. That's a really big positive I think! I get excited for them and encouraged by their actions.

Often we get confused between what we want and what we need and there is a big difference. Wants are superficial. They involve our ego and are possessions. A bigger house, a better car, more jewellery, shoes, handbags – whatever your thing is! All will be well if we have a bigger, better mousetrap but in my experience that couldn't be further from the truth. Needs, on the other hand, are indicative of the important, essential things in life – they pertain to our survival, and our emotional and spiritual health. The horse industry thrives on people's wants. Just have a look at any horse magazine and it will smack you straight between the eyes! 'Do you want your horse to win? Then buy our product, use our shampoo for that winning shine, use our saddle, use our feed, use this bit, buy this float, go to this trainer, etc!' The list goes on and on and it is very emotive. I see so many women who have bought what they were told was the best horse for them, the best gear, the best float and it all looks very flash and paints a pretty, but superficial, picture. What they actually *need*, however, is a safe horse, a safe saddle and some safety tools so they can enjoy their time with their horse and not feel overwhelmed or incompetent. We can get so wound up in what we want that we don't take the time to understand what it is that we need. We must not let our wants override our needs.

By and large, though, as women we are aware of that little voice inside all of us that, if we listen to it, will steer us away from the superficiality of gimmicks and gadgets and guide us towards what is really good for us – what we need. For some it may take a while to figure it out but eventually most of us get there! And when we do our self-worth escalates in the most positive way imaginable.

Our ego is the balancer that enables us to find a healthy level within ourselves, to keep all of these various factors in check. Our self-worth cannot be established by having our ego stroked by someone else; we have to figure it out for ourselves. It took me a long time to realise this. I was so reliant on other people's perceptions of me as a means of identifying myself that I wanted my ego to be stroked. I wanted that attention. I wanted to be told by other people how fantastic I was. I never believed in myself enough to not need this sort of ego stroking. If on the odd occasion I was told I was doing a good job I would take that compliment egotistically but I didn't believe in its sincerity and I was suspicious of the person's motives because I didn't believe in myself and my capabilities.

I needed to find clarity between what I wanted to hear and what I needed to believe. It took me a long time to understand the difference. When I eventually had some understanding, I looked into myself to try to establish who I was. I went in search of my authentic self. I had to define and articulate to myself who I was and who I wanted to be. I had to get the labels out of my life and out of my head. If you have any sort of a fracture in your self-worth and self-belief it can be split open very wide very quickly without too much prodding. The only way I could prevent that and ensure that I continued to grow was to be very sure of who my authentic self was. Up to that point, everything about my self-belief stemmed back to my childhood. When I reflected on that I actually didn't remember having any feelings of self-worth or self-belief as a child. The only thing I did recall was that I was a tomboy, I was sporty and I rode horses a lot. These were activities that gave me some sense of pleasure and satisfaction but they didn't provide me with any form of self-worth. I could not recall going to bed feeling positive and content within myself. Maybe children don't though; perhaps they just live in the moment.

It wasn't easy to revisit the issues of my childhood and teenage years when I began my journey of attaining peace and finding my self-worth and self-identity, but it was necessary to do so. It is often a painful process to review our lives, our actions and the outcomes of those actions. It is a necessity, however, for us to take responsibility for our lives and to take control of who we are and what we want to achieve. In the end the effort is worth it and we are always better off.

Left: My parents in 1954. This is the first time they met at a debutante ball.

Below: My mother and I when I was 18 months old sitting on my grandfather's 1965 Dodge.

Right: I am four years old here, standing beside my father's 1953 Ford Mainline Ute.

Below: Breastfeeding my second child when he was two days old at my mother's house. I was seventeen.

Above: Me at sixteen in my mother's kitchen and having my drink of choice, which in those days was a Claytons and lemonade. The drink you had when you weren't having a drink!

Right: My mother and stepfather at a dance around 1986-1987.

Left: Here I am with my first son when he was eight months old. It was early 1982 when I was eighteen and this picture was taken out at Lake Weeroona in Bendigo on one of my many Sunday visits to the children when they were in foster care.

Below: With my daughter on my wedding day to David, February 29, 1993.

Left: Here I am teaching at a Clinic in 2011.

Below: Explaining something to a participant at a clinic in Ayr, Queensland in 2012.

Photo credit Stacie Robinson

Opposite page above: David and I at home in 2013.

Opposite page below: Equitana in Melbourne 2012 doing a demonstration with my horse Cassidy.

Right: Cassidy and I doing a liberty demonstration at the 2013 'Man from Snowy River Festival' in Jindabyne, New South Wales.

Below: Participants and fence-sitters watching a demonstration at the beginning of a weekend clinic in Sydney 2011.

Photo credit Stacie Robinson

One of the many promotional photos I have had taken over the years. Here I am with Tuscan, my big, beautiful, black warmblood in 2009.

Chapter 13

Anger, being the victim and control

I lived with anger for a long time – anger towards others who I blamed for all the 'wrong doings' in my life and the various situations I found myself in. It was easier to be angry and to blame everyone else than to take a long, hard look in the mirror. If I had bothered to do that with open eyes and honesty, I may have been able to see that I was also accountable for my actions – not everything had been done to me by others!

Living with anger is a symptom of other unresolved emotional issues; so is needing to be in control and allowing yourself to live your life as a victim. Have you ever seen a cornered and terrified dog or horse suddenly become aggressive, even though it is normally a passive, gentle creature? People are no different. Lashing out in anger or harbouring deep-seated, internal bitterness and anger/resentment are symptoms of living a life in fear of being hurt at every level. Fear of being hurt emotionally, fear of being hurt spiritually or fear of being hurt physically.

Sometimes it is the culmination of fear of being hurt on all three levels. All of these are by-products of an overwhelming sense of fear and are very, very destructive.

When you become angry you have often run out of words to express how you feel. Blowing up in anger is an instant form of self-defence. It is also the total and utter end of any form of communication. When someone lashes out verbally in anger, there are lots of words that shouldn't be heeded. Angry outbursts, where you feel a total lack of any ability to communicate, can also be a very valuable learning opportunity. Why are you angry? What are the triggers that make you angry? Is it that you feel you are not being heard? Why aren't you being heard? Anger will never give you a voice in the heat of the moment, it will only inflict pain and hurt upon others. I get really interested when I am angry because I look at what triggers me to feel like this. I'm glad that I feel the emotion of anger sometimes, because it highlights to me what my triggers can be and it gives me the ability to deal with those triggers if they should arise again. If you are prepared to analyse and take a step back from anger it can be a good thing. Conversely, anger can be a very toxic emotion that can bring you and your relationships unstuck in the blink of an eye if you ignore it and do not seek to find out what is really going on underneath.

Fortunately, in my professional life I have only really had one experience with a woman whose anger knew no bounds and it was so deep-seated and dark it was a very sad and distressing thing to see. She came to one of my camps a few years ago and in the morning decided to take her horse out along the road in a halter for a pick of green grass. Her horse was quite ignorant and strong and walked all over her; trained and respectful he was not. A truck went past and spooked him and he pulled back and got away from her. Luckily for her, the horse and any innocent person who may have been driving past at the time, David was close by. He saw what had happened and diverted a potential disaster by stopping the horse from escaping onto the main road where the speed limit was 100 kilometres per hour and massive trucks hurtled backwards and forwards all day long.

When I found out what had happened I was horrified. Late in the morning when the opportunity arose I took her aside. I suggested that she shouldn't do that again until she had put a bridle on her horse and the horse had a whole lot more training under his belt. She looked at me aghast. 'Oh, I don't know what all the fuss is about,' she said. 'He wouldn't have gone out onto the main road, he just got a fright for a minute. He would have come back to me because he loves me!' David and I tried to explain to her in a calm and gentle way that horses do not love us in the same way that we love. They can recognise you, recognise your smell, know your car and feel more comfortable around you than a total stranger but it is not the sort of love she was thinking of. Well, did that strike a sore spot. She was so furious with us she swore at me, promptly got up and left the stables and hid herself away in the bunkhouse for the rest of the day and then packed up and left. She was so angry within herself for some reason, that we became the reason and the trigger for that all to come bubbling back up. I feel sorry for her – it must be terrible to carry that much anger inside you all the time. This reaction was about her as a person and her life. She just used the experience with her horse that day as an excuse to let everything boil over. She would have to dig too deep to really see what was going on and no doubt that would be extremely painful for her. Wherever she is now I hope she has found some peace and has started to heal from whatever it is that has put her in this web of anger and fear.

Fear is self-preservation at its most acute. Unfortunately, anger, the need to be in control and the perpetuation of the victim role in your life are very self-destructive qualities to possess. They are also exhausting to maintain. Anger was a self-protection strategy which in my mind kept me safe from being hurt. In reality it caused a lot more hurt because my anger pushed people away and taught people not to like me or even attempt to get to know me. I was known as 'the angry bitch' in the district. Nothing could be further from the truth. I was in fact frightened and fighting to keep myself together and my head above water. So sad, so very sad that I was misjudged and was at a loss to be able to rectify it for so long.

When I decided to leave Rochester with my two children, the only way I could cope was to maintain the rage and believe I was bigger, braver and better than anything that could be thrown at me. Sounds like a teenager doesn't it? Indestructible, fearless, uncompromising – well that is exactly what I was, a teenager behaving like a teenager. There was one small difference (well, two) – I was a teenager with two tiny children.

I became a control freak, my anger fuelling my determination to get away and show the world I could cope. No-one could do anything better than I could and if they tried they'd muck up and then feel my anger. If when you raise your children you try to control everything and everyone around you, you are doing them an enormous disservice. You are crippling them. They cannot learn by having a go at something, by making mistakes, by having their own successes. A control freak will make sure their children grow up feeling they are never good enough, so why bother even having a go? It is the greatest way of undermining someone's self-belief. You don't even have to verbally criticise, it can just be by your actions – your children will know. After all, if they offer to help and you say 'No I'll do it, it will be quicker anyway' how do you think they would feel? Defeated, worthless, incompetent – I think so. Or if they do something and then see you redoing it, what sort of message does that send?

And what about perpetuating the role of being a victim? At a less obvious level, maintaining this role is a very good way to cover up grief. It may be the grief of losing someone you love or the grief of losing your identity. I allowed my victim hat to stay well and truly in place for many years because of my upbringing and the loss of my family, the loss of my brother and the loss of my unborn child. My dysfunction was everyone else's fault – it was not my fault, I was not to blame.

The women I see who are victims are actually relieved when I can explain back to them what they have expressed to me. They become really interested in the concept that someone sees them and their situation from another perspective. Quite often this will lead to a light bulb moment and they are grateful that a light has been shone on their circumstance and a way forward has presented itself. Others will get angry or even angrier than when they began. It is important to just let them feel that and let them sit with that anger and the intensity of their emotions. There is no right or wrong about this – it just is. If you apply pressure to someone who isn't ready to change, it just makes everything worse. Having some sort of emotional dysfunction isn't open to public opinion or interference. Everyone has different levels of contentment and understanding – it is not for someone else to judge.

I do not give out answers for the women I see. I just try to give them clarity about what they are feeling by talking about my own experiences. When I was at my lowest point all I had was me in all of the turmoil. That is what I see inside of them too, and I try to let them know that I understand because I have been where they are.

Chapter 14

Emotional hangovers

An emotional hangover can lead us to do things, which might be good or bad, that we may not otherwise do. It is a cause and effect thing. Emotional hangovers are often misunderstood and can attack your self-esteem. I see this all the time with the women I teach. Their self-doubt infiltrates their personal life, their riding life and their professional life. They expect themselves to step up and overcome their fears and doubts because that's what they 'used' to do. They do not allow themselves the grace of being kind to themselves and having a think about what their hangover may be. For example, I see many women who used to ride as kids and had plenty of tumbles and falls but would get straight back on, thinking little about it. Now, as mature women with a lifetime of experiences good, bad and ugly, if they have a fall their confidence is shattered. They feel, however, that they should react as they did as children and just get back on or get over it. This is extremely conflicting and confronting for them and they are filled with fear, self-doubt and emotional fragility. The emotional hangover is the fall but it is not a bad thing, it is totally understandable. Every woman is born with a strong instinct for their survival and safety. If they weren't they would not be able to produce and care for the next generation. It is such a primeval part of their womanhood, and combined with their intuition it is very hard to overcome. If you don't know how to improve the 'threatening' situation you are in (in this instance the fear of falling off) then the problem will manifest itself and it will become a stronger and stronger belief until it seems almost insurmountable. In order to change you need to confront yourself with the harsh reality of what your emotional hangover is about or be confronted about it by someone else. Neither option is easy but it is necessary.

An emotional hangover presents itself in stages. First there is a grieving process for what was or what might have been. Next you need to find the time to nurture yourself and be quiet within yourself as you find acceptance and understanding for what you are feeling. Maybe you will be angry about your loss or your 'might haves'; that's okay too. Accept that for what it is and then move on. After this you will need support from people around you. There is no point suffering alone – share your thoughts and help others help you work through the issue/s. Finally, there is a need for change and it is up to you to set out a plan to initiate that change.

Change can be challenging no matter what the circumstances, particularly if you are trying to change self-talk and habits, and push yourself out of your comfort zone. Only the individual themselves can effect change; what is that saying? 'When the student is ready, the master will appear'? A woman at one of my clinics summed it up beautifully: 'If I had known what I was coming to, I wouldn't have come but now I don't want to be anywhere else!' This transpired after a weekend of her sitting quietly, a little shut down and remote, not opening up very much or contributing a great deal to the circle. Like so many others, she thought she was coming to a simple riding clinic to help her regain her confidence as an older woman returning to the saddle. Over the course of the clinic it dawned on her that there was so much more to her confidence issues than she had ever realised. She became engaged in and enthralled by the concept and wanted to learn more so that it would resonate throughout other areas of her life. Once again the safety and acceptance of the other women there helped her reflect upon her own life and she was able to explore things within herself in a calm and loving way and start to unravel some deep-seated and well-practised labels she had put on herself throughout her life, ones she did not feel comfortable wearing any more. The door had been opened, all she had to do was step through it. The student has to be ready and willing in the first place.

If you are not ready for change then you need to be left alone to just let things be. Some of the women I teach need to not be confronted by what it is that has created their emotional hangover in the first place. If they have had a bad fall and lost their confidence because their horse was highly strung and nervous they need to move on from that horse and find a quieter, more placid horse and leave behind the experiences and uncertainties of their previous horse.

If you don't learn from your traumas what is the point? In my experience, women in particular will not change things in their life until their circumstances have hurt them enough. It is as if they feel unworthy of the effort it may take, by them and others, to make the changes necessary to put them in a better, safer place both physically and emotionally. And so the cycle of low self-esteem and self-worth, lack of confidence and being a victim comes full circle.

Chapter 15

A new direction

When I met David he had three horses, a dog, a cat and a budgie and they were all called Jack! His theory was that you call one for dinner and they all arrive. He was born and bred in Drysdale, not far from where we live now. He started riding in novelty events as a child, and when he got to the end of school he didn't know what he was going to do next. His brother applied for a position as a cook up in the Territory so David, with his love of horses, followed him as a stockman. He worked his way through to head stockman and would fly or drive home every wet season; it was on one of these occasions that I met him. After we met he never went back to the Territory.

David then started working as a boat mechanic. In our free time we enjoyed riding and training the horses David owned. He had several quarter horses when I met him and it was really wonderful to have horses back in my life on a regular basis. I hadn't had a horse in my life for years and I had really missed that contact, even though they had never been far from my thoughts.

David also spent some time on the rodeo circuit bronco riding, using the bronco riding and camp-drafting skills he had learnt in the Territory. He gained a reputation for being able to sit on anything; even people in the racing industry would phone and ask him to break in the occasional thoroughbred. We were both working hard to make ends meet and eventually we had saved enough to buy our place in Drysdale, which we called Costalot Park. The word travelled quickly in regard to David's skill as a horseman and we began breaking in and training horses for free. We became so busy it got to the point where every day there would be ten or fifteen people watching us breaking in horses, and one day one of them said to us, 'You know, don't you think it's time you started charging for this?'

David has always been a stickler for getting things right and he always knew the old rough techniques of horse breaking weren't the right way, so he made it his business to find a better way. A friend of ours gave him some videos by American horse-trainer John Lyons. It was raining one day so David came inside to watch them. He played the tapes over and over and then practised what he had seen. Eventually we were asked to do our first symposium, a night demonstration on the other side of Geelong. David had to start working with an unbroken horse to get it to a point where it could be bridled, saddled and ridden within a few hours, which he did. I was so nervous that I sat on the Esky and drank way too much! Back then I didn't speak to people because, in my view, it had nothing to do with me, I was just there as David's wife.

Eventually David quit his job as a boat mechanic and began to train horses pretty much full-time. He occasionally drove concrete trucks to fill in but mostly he trained horses. I was always working at something, managing a stud or agistment facility or some other form of employment, to bring in extra cash.

David began teaching people and as the business grew we realised we either had to get very professional about what we were doing or not do it at all. I wrote to John Lyons in the United States. He has an accreditation program over there but it takes two years to get through it. It took me a year to get an answer from him but I finally did and John said he would come off the road and work with David one-on-one for six weeks. In those days the exchange rate was only 47 cents to the dollar, so although we had the go-ahead from John we were two people with a young family and a mortgage and it seemed almost impossible to do. However, as soon as people around town heard about what we wanted to do and the opportunity David had been given to work with John, they started organising fundraising nights for us, which helped us raise some money. It wasn't a lot but it was enough to get our airfares together.

I spoke with John's office and they agreed to put us on a payment plan. I think the total cost for us to do the training program was $38,000 and our income for that year was only $19,000! We were taking on a huge debt and a huge risk but we went anyway. We had our friends look after the children at home and we went for six weeks. John was completely blown away by how established David was in his horsemanship and his horse-training, and John had just as good a time as David did. What John taught David was how to teach. David already had a good handle on training, and of course they added a lot more to it together, but it was fantastic that John gave David the confidence to teach.

Now David and John are best friends. David was the best man at John's wedding. Their relationship is based on more than horse-training; they are good friends with a mutual admiration and respect for one another as professionals and men. The decision we made to go to America and the friendship that was founded as a result has been an important part of our life, our business and what we are doing today.

Both David's and John's training has evolved. They don't see each other a lot so they develop training ideas separately, and every time we visit the US it's great to see the dynamics of their training methods. It's really wonderful to see how much they love each other. They adore each other's company and I think it's good for John to have someone like David who is close to him, just as it is great for David to have a mentor who doesn't have an ego and is very easy to be around.

When we were over in the States, John told David that he should stay in America as he would have the opportunity to make a ton of money due to his talent. Tempting as it was, David and I have always known that we are Australian through and through and this is where we belong. There was also no way we could turn our back on everyone in Australia who had helped and supported us. We've had many an opportunity to go to the States and work but it's not about the money, it's about changing lives; changing horses' lives, changing people's lives and we decided at the time to take the opportunity to do that here in Australia. Our children were still young and we didn't want to be away from them or disrupt their lives, their schooling and friendships by travelling backwards and forwards to America. Now that they are all independent young adults we have been given the opportunity to work at clinics and symposiums over there, which we are really excited about, though we would never contemplate moving there permanently because we would miss our family and friends too much. The thought of travelling on long flights doesn't bother me at all because sitting on a plane for me means rest! The phone doesn't ring and nobody can get hold of me.

It would be great for our business to expand into the enormous market in America. From the reaction of the American women I've spoken to, they are all amazed and interested in the training I do, dealing with women and their confidence issues. As far as I can ascertain there doesn't seem to be anyone over there teaching these women. Women all over the world are no different from the women in Australia with their lack of confidence. My message and my training methods have flown around pretty quickly amongst the horsey women of America and that's what it's all about, getting the message out. I think my life is ready for that challenge and I think David is ready for that too.

When we came back from the first time with John Lyons we realised we could make a profession out of what we had already been doing. We started to charge for what we were doing. I was still working at whatever I could find to do here and there but we poured everything into running

David's business. He was the sole focus of our business and I was so proud of him. I knew how talented he was as a horse-trainer and I was happy to see him spread his wings and show other horse enthusiasts this talent. I went with him to clinics and demonstrations, helping organise things behind the scenes, talking to people, answering the queries and so on. Things were about to change for me, though, at Equitana 2003.

Chapter 16

The message gets out

Finally returning to the saddle after many years' absence, I was devastated to find I had lost confidence in my riding. I felt like a fool. After all, I was the kid who used to ride anything. But try as I might I could not find that kid any more. She had gone with the responsibility of being a mother and the passing of time, coupled with some pretty major confidence knocks along the way. The added complication to this was that I was married to David, who was a wonderful horse-trainer; people would simply say, 'Oh, you're so lucky because if you have a problem with your horse you can just get David to fix it for you!' This made me feel worse – I felt more inadequate, more incapable. What little shred of self-belief and self-respect I had for my riding was torn to pieces with constant comments like this. In my mind I heard the chatter: 'You're not capable or competent enough to figure this out so give the horse to someone who can!' I was determined to overcome what at the time seemed to me an illogical fear, so I asked David to help me develop a training method specifically for my concerns. And my number one concern was getting on the horse and riding it. The 'what ifs' would kick in. 'What if he shies? What if I come off? What if I get hurt?' There is nothing worse, no matter how experienced or confident you are, than being on a horse knowing they are not paying attention to you and feeling that 'any minute' these things could happen – it sends shivers up my spine even thinking about it!

David always starts out doing groundwork with his horses. His philosophy is, 'Why would you get on a horse who is jumpy, distracted and not paying attention to you on the ground? It is only going to get worse when you are mounted.' This makes perfect sense to me but we are taught to just get on the horse and ride, and the concept of groundwork is almost seen as a form of wimpishness or incompetence by some individuals who are less enlightened than others! We also took into consideration that I wanted to have some rock-solid safety tools in my repertoire to fall back on, both emotionally and physically, if the need arose. Horses are at their strongest when they have their body in a straight line. This is when they can use maximum physical effort to bolt, buck or rear – all the things which you definitely don't want to happen. To have a method of stopping this happening is a great piece of armoury you have in your training.

Next we developed a series of exercises to practise on the ground initially, that could also be used when the horse is being ridden. This started out with the 'hip-over' cue (where the horse disengages its hindquarters, places its inside leg over and under its body and turns in a small circle with its neck flexed to the inside), the walk-forward cue, shoulder-over cue and rein-back cue. These can be used individually or strung together in any particular order to train your horse on the ground. By practising these over and over again you are also training yourself to really think about what you are doing and where you are asking your horse to place its feet. You learn that timing and your own body control is a crucial element in making it work.

The other aspect of training I needed to explore was how to teach a horse patience. As soon as I put my foot in the stirrup I didn't want the horse to start to move around and attempt to walk off – that was just downright dangerous. I wanted my horse to stand still beside a mounting block for as long as it took to get myself organised (or pluck up the courage) to get on; no matter how clumsily or undignified my mounting might be the horse would have to stand there as still as a rock and be patient!

With these simple methods I found I became very involved and committed to my training, which in turn gave me something to work towards. I developed a sense of achievement and competence as I saw the benefit of the work I was putting in. There were two offshoots of this: I didn't feel pressured to ride if I didn't want to, because I was still spending time with my horse training him; and my confidence grew and grew and I wanted to learn more and felt capable of taking more on. It was fantastic! It didn't occur to me at the time that it would be of any relevance or interest to anyone else. I was doing this purely for my own benefit.

I was totally unprepared for what was about to happen to me in 2003. David was at Equitana, the world's largest horse exhibition and trade fair, as an educator and demonstrator. We had our booth in the trade village and I was helping behind the scenes, talking to the general public and 'manning' our stand. One day out of the blue my friend Colleen, who works for Equitana, came to our booth. She asked me if I was ready to give a demonstration and if so I needed to be at such and such a point by such and such a time! '*What?* Are you kidding?' I said.

'Why not?' said Colleen. 'Just go and do what you do and I am sure it will all fall into place!' I was gobsmacked and in virtually no time at all there I was standing in the middle of the demonstration arena with my horse, Galli, whom we had brought along to be used in the Cowboy Dressage demonstration that David was doing. I was miked up and the show was due to begin! I had never done any public speaking before so as I looked out at the crowd I took a deep breath and decided that all I could do was to be frank and honest with everyone and explain to them what it was that I did with my horse and why.

'Hi everyone,' I began, 'my name is Sandi Simons and I am petrified when I ride my horse!' There was a brief hush from the crowd as if they were digesting what they had just heard. Did they hear what they thought they had? Yes, indeed, and then quite spontaneously I got a standing ovation. I went on to explain that for many people my lack of confidence was hard to understand as I hadn't had a nasty fall off a horse. My lack of confidence was because I had had five children over the years and had been out of the saddle for a long time. The fearless child who used to ride anything had grown up and had developed a sense of her own mortality and vulnerability, but I was still desperate to ride and be around horses. Their reaction confirmed to me that I was on the right track and that maybe I really did have something to share.

When I had finished I was bombarded with questions and people coming up and saying 'Thank you for your brutal honesty, it is such a relief to know that I am not alone. I am also scared when I ride and I feel like such a fool and a failure.' I never knew there were so many women out there who felt the same way I did.

When I got back to our booth, Colleen informed me that she had ten people already confirmed for my first clinic. Excuse me? What clinic? Unbeknown to me she had made up Expression of Interest and Registration forms, working on one of her hunches that people would want to hear what I had to say and would want to learn more.

Five or six weeks after Equitana I conducted my first Confidence Clinic in Gisborne, Victoria. On my way to the location I was really excited. I had an overwhelming sense of validation. The kid and young woman who had never been heard, whom no-one had ever bothered to pass the time of day with or seek an opinion from, who had only ever been criticised and made to feel worthless and small, finally had people who wanted to listen to what she had to say. They were interested in me, they were interested in my message. I had something to contribute. I was valued for my opinions – I had a voice.

I didn't have a plan for this clinic; I still don't really for any of the clinics or camps. It is something that just unfolds. If you look on my website you will see what the overall plan for a Confidence Camp is on a day-by-day basis but it is not set in stone. I prefer to let the clinics and camps unfold in an organic way. I believe that you cannot run to a script with what I do – you just have to go with the feel around you, moment by moment. If you have a plan you may well aquaplane over someone who needs to be quiet within herself. One particular clinic or camp participant may need more quiet time on a one-to-one basis. My antenna is always up and I am constantly gauging and assessing what is going on around me so that I can best help the women who come along. The natural balance of the clinics and camps always reveals itself. Everyone wants to be heard no matter who they are or where they are in life. Everyone has a voice and has something to contribute. It is really important to me that everyone's voice and opinion is listened to, really listened to not just heard.

There is always someone in particular who stands out at every clinic and camp I conduct. These are the women I usually learn the most from. They can be very complex and bring with them a whole cavalcade of challenges and emotions. And that very first clinic in Gisborne was no exception. Initially she appeared to be the ringleader. She had a strong presence about her but when I looked a little closer I could also sense a vulnerability that she was frightened to expose. Her horse, as they always do, held the key to what was going on deep within her. He was fearful and tense, unsure as to what was expected of him and full of conflict. He was exhibiting a range of behaviours that would suggest a jumbled dialogue of mixed messages. He was mirroring his owner's mental and emotional state. I had a feeling that it would take a while for me to be able to walk alongside her and help her because if I did this too soon she would probably feel confronted and offended. If I didn't pick my time with her, there was no doubt in my mind she would have been hurt. It was a potentially volatile situation.

Many times people have asked me how I do what I do. I don't know, really. It is just a feeling I have. It is as if I have a mirror and while I am looking at the person I am looking at myself. This is what gives me, I believe, a level of understanding for what women are going through. I am looking at them through my own eyes and my own experiences. I do not judge them, I do not form an opinion. They don't have to explain anything to me as I have been there too.

I kept an eye on this woman for the whole weekend and I assessed her horse as a separate issue. Her horse was scary and out of control. His bad behaviour was very intimidating. When I felt the time was right I said to her, 'I really don't want you to ride this horse. It is not about him, it is about you and your future. I can offer you some solutions to this though.' And so I proceeded to explain her options to her and what solutions she may be able to find. As soon as I said this, her sense of relief was palpable. The layers she had put up to protect herself emotionally peeled away one by one. She knew that I knew. There was no more battling on alone. She had found an ally and a friend in her battle with herself and her battle with her horse.

When I drove home from that first clinic I was exhausted but I was so proud of myself. I was also really excited as I felt that I was about to change not only my life but that of my family and those of many, many women who all thought they were alone. I couldn't wait for the next clinic!

News spreads quickly in the horse world and it wasn't too long until the next Confidence Clinic was full. And the next. It has continued to gain momentum and evolve ever since. David and I are now away most weekends around Australia and hold half a dozen live-in camps, mainly at our home in Drysdale, each year as well. I help women with specific issues they have with their horses and David continues to train performance horses and riders who want to gain more knowledge and achieve that winning edge in their chosen discipline. We are busier than we ever imagined after spending that time with John Lyons.

Chapter 17

The first Confidence Camp

Early in 2006 I was conducting a weekend Confidence Clinic in Tyabb, Victoria, when one of the women there said at the end of the weekend, 'I wish I could come home with you and stay for a month – there is so much more I want to learn!' I was happy she had enjoyed herself and felt some real benefit from having come to the clinic.

Her comments got me thinking on the way home and I thought 'Well, why not? It shouldn't be too hard to extend a two-day clinic into a five-day live-in experience.' So, after I had been conducting my Confidence Clinics for two and a half years I decided to offer Confidence Camps – a five-day, live-in 'getaway' for women and their horses – which initially were held exclusively at our home. With my mind racing I thought about what facilities we had at home that would make it possible. There were plenty of horse facilities: stables, yards, a round yard, arena – the horse side of the accommodation was easy and all taken care of. What about the people? Aha! If our son moved out of the bungalow – which he had said that he was thinking of doing – then we could convert the bungalow into living quarters for the women. I really like to have about six women at a camp as this means it is intimate enough for everyone to feel involved and included and it is easier to work closely with them in their training. I rang David on the way home, excited by this new venture. Bless his heart, he listened to me babble on in his usual calm, thoughtful manner and said, 'Yeah, why not? I can ask so-and-so to help give me a hand and I am sure you can get cracking on the interior and the decorating.' With that, we were off and running and six or seven weeks later the very first Confidence Camp was held in May 2006.

In the ensuing weeks I thought long and hard about what I would like if I went away for a holiday with my horse. First of all I would want to be educated – I would want to know more about those vague things people talk about when you first start riding or are getting back into riding. Things like horse dentistry, saddle-fitting and horse nutrition. The fact that I was at a Confidence Camp meant I would want to learn more about my horse and my relationship with it, and start learning how I could increase my confidence and my level of competency. From a personal point of view, being a busy mum, not having to think about going anywhere near a supermarket or even think about a meal would be hedonistically divine! And if I really wanted to push the 'all-about-me' factor then why not throw in a facial and a massage? *Heaven!* The whole week needed, I thought, to encapsulate calm, uninterrupted time with your horse where there were no deadlines, no pressures of day-to-day living. In a way it should feel a bit like being a kid again over the summer holidays – hanging out with your friends, endless time with your horse and not a care in the world.

Primarily, though, it was all about safe training. If the opportunity presented itself then there could be some exposure to other situations so that by the time the participants went home they didn't have to worry about going out with their horse. The women who come to my camps end up going trail riding at the pony club, down to the nearby beach and sometimes over to an indoor arena. They put themselves and their horses in situations they may not feel confident enough to tackle on their own but really do want to have a go at. It is all done in a safe and nurturing environment to help them with their confidence. The camp also covers a variety of questions such as whether their saddle fits, how their horse is travelling, their horse's health and whether his/her teeth are okay; we even get right down to float loading for women.

The night before everyone arrived for that first camp, surprisingly I wasn't nervous, I was really excited. I knew all but two of the six women who were coming as they had been to my Confidence Clinics before. As the week unfolded it was truly amazing what was revealing itself. There was so much love, fun and energy amongst these women it was inspiring. They were all from totally different backgrounds and all had had different horse experiences. The cross-section of the group was fairly typical of what I see in most of my clinics and camps. There were women who had decided that, now that their family was all grown up and there was a bit more time available, they might fulfil their childhood dream and learn how to ride; there were women who'd had a long break from riding and had decided to get back in the saddle; there were women who'd had a fright or a fall which had rocked their confidence; there were women who just had the wrong horse and this gave them a bad feeling – a sense of being out of control physically and emotionally. Some were very experienced horsewomen, others were absolute rookies. They all shared that common bond, horses. They also shared the quiet knowledge that they had reached a crossroads in their life, an intangible, barely realised concept that they were about to embark on a journey with one another that would forever bond them. This is what I find most inspiring and mystical – I can best describe it as the coming together of kindred spirits, the unique and enveloping comfort of the emotional strength of women, the sisterhood of women. It is the life force of the human species as ancient as time, which will forever be interwoven into our physical, emotional and spiritual beings. Being able to assist women with their horse-training as well as their personal development was intoxicating and exciting.

I have several wonderful assistants who help me at my clinics and camps. Each one of them has been an important addition to the team as they bring with them their own unique set of qualities. Some of them are very experienced horsewomen with a lifetime of knowledge and riding behind them. Others are latecomers who buy a horse, learn a whole different set of skills and more often than not find they have some confidence issues along the way! I love integrating them and their teaching into the camps and clinics and I know the participants love their compassion, strength, knowledge and humour because they have told me so!

I am pretty sure I can say my assistants and I learn from one another all the time and we make a great team. You always need more than one set of eyes at the camps and clinics and I know we complement one another with our personal, life and horsemanship skills. As a team we are able to deliver the best possible experience for all who attend. Being able to work with women as genuine and caring as they are and have their friendship is a gift. My time on the road is never the same without David but when he isn't there I really appreciate having such wonderful support and companionship from the girls!

The first Confidence Camp came to a close and I was really proud of myself. I know that sounds cocky and arrogant but it was certainly a unique emotion for me to feel. Through the turbulence of the first part of my life and the ever-present sense of never being good enough or important enough, pride and a sense of self-esteem and self-worth were foreign to me. I know the women had a wonderful time – you could see it in their eyes, their spirits lifted as they left with a sense of accomplishment and fulfilment. A couple of them verbalised as much before they left. For a bit of fun one of them suggested there should be a visitors book where people could write their thoughts before they left. Somehow or other the blank walls of the bungalow's bathroom became the visitors book. It has become a camp tradition to write on the walls and they are chock-a-block with various messages from the women who have come to the camps over the years.

I was keen to know what everyone had thought of the week. I asked them to write down something about themselves if they wanted to, and about why they came, how they felt and what they felt they would take away with them. I received this the following week from one of the participants.

The concept of me being a nervous rider must have been quite bizarre for anyone looking from the outside in. I was surrounded by horses every day – I handled them, bridled them, fed them, rugged them. Would teach them to load onto floats, learn to tie up etc. I traipsed around the state with my daughter doing the pony club and interschool circuit at the time. I had been competing myself not so very long ago with some success. But then my darling faithful, well-educated horse retired and I had a series of unsuitable horses after that; so there I was surrounded by horses of my own on our property which had been all set up for horses with a major confidence issue! Yikes! Help! Yes indeed, I needed help! I couldn't really verbalise what it was that made me want to keep finding a way to overcome my fear – why is it that time and time again women who love horses, even though they are scared, keep wanting to have them in their life?

Even as I write this it seems illogical. People who have never liked horses or have never had the opportunity to get to know a horse would not understand and who can blame them? If I was reading about or listening to someone who was absolutely terrified of heights and yet kept being drawn to go skydiving even though it rattled them to their very core, making them feel sick with nerves, I'd think they had rocks in their head and I know I would be thinking to myself 'Why would they put themselves through this?'

However, as crazy as it sounds that is just the way it is and so one day I was in our local Horseland store and saw an ad on the notice board for a weekend Confidence Clinic you were holding locally. I had heard something about you and what you did, Sandi – I don't know where and I don't recall why but it was enough of a prompt for me to write the number down and ring the coordinator. I asked if observers (or fence-sitters as I now know they are called) could come. 'Sure,' she said. 'Don't you have a horse?' 'Yes I do but I would rather come and watch as I have only just got him.' 'This would be the perfect opportunity to bring him along and get you two started on your journey together,' was her reply. Well, why not? And so on Saturday I loaded up the 17-hands-high, 8-year-old just off-the-track (literally) ex-steeplechaser and arrived at the clinic! Boy did I do a lot of talking to myself to boost my courage on the way down there! Am I nuts? Yes probably but these were desperate times and desperate measures had to be taken!

He clattered off the float but was really very good. I had no idea what to expect and I was so relieved when I was told to put him in a yard and make myself a cup of tea! Six or seven women sat around the table that morning out in the sunshine. I didn't know which one was you until you introduced yourself and your assistant trainer Annie. I found it really interesting that you took the time at the beginning of the day to ask us all to share a little bit about ourselves and the reasons why we were there. It was very comforting listening to other people's stories. The individual stories I don't really remember but they had a common theme — middle-aged mums and women wanting to ride but too ashamed to admit how frightened they were and not really understanding why they just couldn't give up on their dreams to get back on a horse. There was no pressure, no peering down noses, no lack of understanding … the whole atmosphere was one of comfort, safety, security and a wonderful sense of discovery and enlightenment. I was taken aback by everyone's honesty, I must admit. I had come from an upbringing where you just did not discuss such personal feelings with total strangers. You never let your guard down and let someone see your vulnerabilities. Nor was it considered ladylike to talk too much about yourself because no-one was really that interested in you and you were not that important! Sounds like something out of the Dark Ages or the way the Royal Family conducts themselves, doesn't it? Well, that is not too far from the truth!

I have to admit, too, that initially I found your ability to hold a mirror up to each one of us a little confronting for all of the same reasons. In my world, people were polite to one another, never showed too much emotion, were never disagreeable, argumentative or contrary — it was just not done! It was considered the height of bad manners to question what people were saying or even suggest that maybe they were not being entirely honest with themselves! I had never met anyone like you before in real life. It was as if you had stepped off the stage from the Dr Phil or Oprah show!

Just before lunch on Saturday I felt I had a handle on the groundwork that you had been showing us. It was all very new to me and my horse Nauto but we did okay. By Sunday I got on – I have to say that again to reinforce in my mind the euphoria and utter amazement I felt. By Sunday I got on! I sat on top of a calm, relaxed horse – a horse that had been galloping around a track winning races not so very long before. I cannot even really put into adequate words the emotion that was welling up inside me … little did I know that the phone call I had made a couple of days before was going to change my life in the most profound ways imaginable.

This time last week I was standing in the pitch dark at 5.45 am in the cold with a horse that refused to get on the float. I was having second thoughts about coming to see you again, at your first week-long camp. In a panic as I had to get on the 7 o'clock ferry, I ran down to the house and woke my husband from a deep and peaceful slumber. He was not at all horsey but this was a desperate situation. With his presence the culprit of all of this turmoil thought better than to misbehave again and walked placidly onto the float, making me feel even more of a fool than previously! When he was finally on board we set off to the ferry. I was sick with nerves and anxiety – what on earth was I doing going to some unknown place with unknown women to stay the week riding? I seriously thought about getting off the ferry, turning around and going back home again; however, I rallied what little courage I had left to muster and soldiered on.

Upon arriving at your place there was not a soul around until a sweet, rosy-faced lady came out to greet me. 'Hello' she said with a big, warm, welcoming smile. 'I'm Carol. Put your horse in here in the stables and I'll show you the bungalow. We are the first ones here.' She obviously knew her way around and so I did what I was told. Eventually the other ladies appeared and the day started. You used the same technique you had done at the clinic, starting out with a relaxed cuppa sitting around a table and asking each one of us to tell a little about ourselves and what brought us there. (Phew, no horse involvement yet I silently thought to myself.) There was no time limit, no sense of being rushed. It took as long as it took.

I recognised one of your assistants from the clinic, who was also there to help. Just as in any situation when strangers come together and then start talking a bit about themselves there were some ladies who were very verbal and others who were more reluctant to open up. I noticed there was a box of tissues on the table ... it wasn't long until they were in use. The tears flowed for some of us that day as we recounted our feelings of helplessness, our long-lost self-esteem and confidence with our horses and our riding. I remember you saying to me 'And whose fault is that?' when I was talking about how I felt as if I was sitting on the sidelines of my life watching everyone else participating except me. Well I had every excuse – I feel bad about taking time out for me; I have four children born close together; my husband is away a lot; my upbringing makes me feel selfish and uncomfortable doing what I want to do; my father instilled in me 'Do the things you have to do first, then you can do the things you want to do', but I am never finished with the things I have to do – the list was endless! As I blurted out all of these excuses I felt like I was a complete looney! You just looked at me and I knew you knew I was running out of reasons not to live my life the way I should and said I wanted to! I had also had some really nasty falls off horses over the years. Various bouts of concussion, broken bones and eventually many years later three prolapsed discs in my neck, which paralysed my left arm and required emergency surgery to stop the paralysis continuing into my legs. For some bizarre reason I still wanted to ride but my confidence was in my boots.

Each one of us had a reason to be there. It was as if by coming to this camp the white flag had been put up and any thread of bravery, competence and fun had been relinquished – snuffed out even; this was the last-ditched stand, the last attempt to overcome the crippling fear and anxiety we were perplexed and paralysed by in our aspirations to ride and enjoy our horses. Well, this is my perspective upon reflection of that first morning; I cannot attest to what others were thinking. Was this going to be the next step in finding that magic panacea to cure me of all my anxiety about actually fulfilling my dreams by continuing to gain more and more knowledge and having the courage to ride more often?

After telling our stories, we went outside to watch you give a demonstration in the round yard with Beau. I was keen to go in and have a turn round-penning – inside turns, outside turns, controlling speed. Sounds easy – it wasn't! Each one of us had a turn. Some were better than others. Some were totally out of their comfort zone and ended up bawling their eyes out standing in the middle of the round yard looking defeated and overwhelmed! You explained to us that round-penning a horse was a reflection of what is going on within us. The horse feels our emotion and mirrors it back to us. If we are uptight and have high energy levels that horse will fly around that round pen and will take absolutely no notice of what we are asking it to do. It wants to get as far away from us as possible. If we are defeated and void of any enthusiasm or spark the horse will either just stand there or saunter around the round pen doing its own thing, totally ignoring our presence. I was enthralled by what was unfolding before me. I could see how a lot of what the women had been expressing about how they felt and why they were at the camp was being exhibited in the round pen. I also had the sense that there was in one or two of the ladies, including myself, more of what had not been said too!

Your patience and guidance were very comforting – you never made anyone feel rushed, incompetent or worried. You seem to have this unique ability to be by someone's side when they need you the most – it is truly a gift. I'm not sure whether you know that or not so I thought I should tell you.

I really liked the way, over the course of the week, we had the opportunity to travel at our own pace and to learn how to keep ourselves safe and feeling competent and in control through the extensive groundwork which translated into ridden work when, and only when, we felt we were ready The various professionals who came in to talk to us about saddle-fitting, horse dentistry and horse nutrition were interesting too and very educational. It was so lovely to be pampered and fussed over when we were with our horses and also when the horses were back in the stables at night time. I had never been away on my own from my family and husband in twenty years of marriage – it was quite a treat! I was just me – not anyone's wife, mother, daughter, sister, canteen volunteer, chauffeur, footy mum, scout mum, pony club mum, nippers mum, I was not a farmer. There were no expectations put on me – I revelled in it and I learnt so much.

When you told us on the second day that we were going to take our horses down the road on a 'trail ride' I had an army of butterflies thrashing themselves around in my stomach. Thankfully it was not the sort of trail ride I expected. I loved (and was so grateful) that first of all it was out of the arena and down the drive – all using groundwork, not under saddle. Eventually when we built up to doing it again under saddle I was so busy concentrating on doing what I had learnt and keeping myself and my horse busy I had no time to be nervous, no time to fill my head with the 'what ifs'!

My moment of truth – my light bulb moment, the highlight of my week – was when we were down at the local pony club and my horse was so over-adrenalised with emotion I wasn't anywhere near getting on him so I was groundworking him to the point of exhaustion (mine, not his). I'll never forget that moment when you came over to me and said 'Stop doubting what you are doing and give yourself some credit – you are not just a rider, you have a gift, you are a horse-trainer and you are damned good at it!' I could have kissed you with relief – it wasn't so much what you said but you had given me permission to not conform to the expectations of the horse world I had grown up in and to explore my own journey without fear of recrimination or disapproval. I was a 'trainer' and I was answerable only to myself and the horses whose lives I hoped to influence in a positive and constructive way.

I had the time of my life. The door has been opened, the light shines brightly. I went out to dinner with other horsey friends from that 'other life' last night, and having what I learnt the previous week still clearly in my mind I heard all their familiar stories – of shying, pig-rooting, badly behaved horses that were all having excuses made for them. And the feeling was that it was perfectly okay for their horses to be like this. After all, the most important thing is to get on them and 'ride them through it'! I know I have had a glimpse of something special, the missing link for all my years with horses. I feel at peace with myself at many different levels, not just in relation to my horses but in other aspects as well. I know I do not have to put myself in that position again, of riding a horse through anything. There is no pressure, it is up to me. When I am ready, not when other people tell me I am ready. I know the horse or horses will tell me and when something does go wrong I am building a solid foundation on the ground with my horse to know how to deal with it, circumnavigate it or diffuse it altogether before it even starts. Oh what a relief! What a long, overdue, blessed relief!

It was a challenging, emotional week. I loved the way you read us all so well Sandi, you have a unique talent to be able to tap into someone's fears and stresses, sometimes before they even realise them themselves. I loved the way we all shared our emotions, laid it out on the table every morning – that was great. This enabled everyone to sit and think, debrief and regroup, and gird our loins for the upcoming day. There was not one cross word, not one bad thought, nothing but support and encouragement from everyone for everyone. How often does that happen in life, that total strangers can come together and share all of this without someone being the rotten apple and undermining the group? Hats off to a special group of ladies; I *look forward to keeping in touch with them and coming together again in six months.*

I am so glad I picked up that phone a couple of months ago and made the call to come to your Tyabb clinic. I would still have been mucking around, confused, undermined, discouraged and aimless with the most beautiful creatures that God has put on this earth! Trying to find that something, knowing that I hadn't but desperately wanting to fill in the missing pieces in the jumble of a jigsaw puzzle I had been pushing around in my head for all of these years. Thank you! Thank you! Thank you! I am so grateful for the gift you have given me!

It was great to receive such feedback from the first Confidence Camp. The other emails I received were very complimentary as well. It was pretty apparent to me that it had been a massive success and I was absolutely delighted. The word spread quite quickly and now I hold somewhere between five to seven Confidence Camps each year. Most weekends I am on the road teaching all over Australia. There are always new faces coming; there are also familiar faces too, and it is always nice to see them again. Some of the participants choose to extend what they have learnt and join David's Trainers Program, a two-year course he has developed for the more serious horsemen and women out there who want to hone their skills and train or ride at a higher level.

In February 2013, I held my first Trainers Program, which is quite different from the one David has been conducting for some years now. I have specifically designed the program for women to learn how to do what I do, so that they can go out and help other women with their horse journey. The first year of the program is working with me and the second year is working with David.

Throughout all of this my rock and my mentor has been David. I am able to bounce training ideas off him and when I get stuck with a training concept he is able to help me. I know as a man he doesn't quite get the 'female' thing! Why would he? But his calm, reassuring encouragement lifts me up and inspires me to be better at what I do every day. I count my blessings that he is in my life as there is no doubt he was the reason I was able to take a good look at myself and turn my life around. David's approval and pride in me and what I am doing is paramount to my success. I know it is the same with him. We are a great team and we complement one another beautifully at every level. I know how very fortunate I am that I happened to be going down those stairs and spilt a drink on him all those years ago!

Chapter 18

The horses, women and me

Throughout all the ups and downs of my life (but especially the downs), horses have been my abiding passion and I have a thirst for knowledge of anything to do with them. I have found as many do that my love of horses and the time I spend with them is good for my soul. They have always been that special something I gravitate towards just for me. There were many years before I met David that I had virtually no contact with a horse at all. I had other priorities raising my children and looking after them. I didn't have the money, the time or the support to own a horse. This didn't stop me from reading everything I could get my hands on to broaden my knowledge and feed the burning passion I had. I have used my interest in horses to keep me emotionally sane throughout my life. I knew that they would always be waiting for me because they have always been such an important part of my life.

When I started out with the clinics and camps I had no idea where this particular part of my life would take me. I understood that what was unfolding before me was not just about women having confidence issues with their riding and the sort of relationship they had with the horse. I knew from my own experience that even though we often don't recognise it, a lack of confidence in one area of our lives can infiltrate other parts. You can raise your head up after years of bringing up a family and having little time for yourself, you can suffer the trauma of being a rape victim, can come out of prison or come out of an abusive relationship, but when you do you are left with a mere shadow of the woman you were before. Some of these experiences will no doubt take away your autonomy and self-worth; others might just wear you out emotionally and spiritually. Women need to give themselves permission to accept themselves for who they are and where they have come from – after all, what has gone before determines who we are today. Even so, many of us are unsure how to go about changing our lives, about how to grow and live the best life we possibly can.

At the clinics and camps women start to realise that they are able to make choices for themselves. There are no roles that need to be played, there are no expectations about who they are, what they have or where they have come from. The clinics and camps are a safe environment for all sorts of concepts to come up and be thrashed around in conversation. It is about bringing kindred spirits together and forming a common bond. We don't have this opportunity very often in today's society.

Women come to the clinics thinking it's about trust for them as a horse rider but it really isn't, it's so much more than that. It's about trusting themselves to take control and to change. People come up to me at Equitana or other places wanting to know what it was that enabled me to learn what I have and why I want to share this with others. The camps and clinics give women a safe place to share and to find out that they are not alone or that they're not abnormal. In sharing their stories and experiences there is invariably a collective surprise that other women feel the same way and then a sigh of relief: 'Thank God, I'm normal, I'm not the only one.' They are given the emotional freedom to explore these feelings further instead of hiding them away or shelving them somewhere in the recesses of their mind. Shelving things is appropriate at times; maybe it's not the right time to deal with something or there isn't a safe space to deal with it. But if that goes on for too long, that 'thing' will rear its ugly head again, often when you least expect it. The sharing and camaraderie between the women is great and I learn so much from them. They get so much from one another in their openness and trust through a common bond of loving horses and riding.

Everyone's natural inclination in conversations is to insert their own opinion. We are always wanting to 'stick our two bob's worth in', cutting people off or thinking ahead to what we're going to say. This need to get our viewpoint across gets in the way of really listening to a person without an agenda. When you stop and listen with a quiet mind, you really get in touch with what that person is saying and how they are feeling. You are able to listen with empathy and understanding. Sometimes you just have to put yourself and your opinions out of the equation. It can be really challenging to do, as it involves putting our ego to one side and not hearing what we want to hear but listening to what is being said. When I was younger I was really good at hearing what I thought people were saying and jumping to conclusions, rather than listening to what was actually been said. David and I decided at one of the early clinics to really listen to our clients and make a special effort not to talk about ourselves and our own experiences. It was quite a challenge to teach people and not talk about yourself and your experiences in the process. When we took this approach we learnt more about our students than we ever had before and that in turn taught us more about ourselves.

My New Year's resolution for the last eight years has been to learn to listen better because I don't think we do enough of it. I deliberately start every day of my clinics and camps with the circle, so that the women can be heard by everyone. Everyone has the right to be heard. It doesn't matter what your story is, whether it takes you ten minutes or half an hour to tell it. You can talk till the cows come home but if you're not listened to, really listened to, there's no point.

People are worth listening to. If someone is talking to me and sharing their experiences with me I see that as an enormous privilege. I feel very honoured that someone is even remotely interested in sharing their story with me. It's not an imposition on my time, it's a gift. Some days I don't want to listen because I feel I have listened and listened and my ears are red raw from listening and that's okay too. Sometimes I just want to listen to me! But I choose my times appropriately. Sometimes I like my own company and sometimes sitting down over coffee with two or three girlfriends is more valuable than any counselling session I'll ever pay for.

Throughout my life I have learnt it is really important to try to gather the right people around you. They have to be good people who share the same moral code and attitudes as you. Good men and women who are emotionally and mentally healthy and stable. These are the ones who are good for your soul. I do my very best to surround myself with these positive influences and stay well clear of what I refer to as 'toxic' people. From time to time I have found a few toxic people in my life and I have been forced to do a cull. Sometimes you have to assess your friendships and relationships and have the courage to cut the negative people out of your life. This is an important part of emotional and spiritual growth. I am continually surrounded by people but there is just a handful who I really let into my personal life. They are people who are good for me and who help me just as much as I like to think I help them.

Chapter 19

What's it all about?

I am not qualified in anything. I left school at age fourteen and was never tempted to return to study as many adults are. I am terrified of taking tests or exams. In fact, when I went for my truck licence I asked the examiner if I could do the written section orally! I have no academic qualifications but my life has, I believe, qualified me in many ways for what I am doing today with my work. I never offer myself as any sort of therapist or someone with all the answers. I have often referred people to professionals if I feel they need to pursue that avenue. What I do have to offer, though, is a lifetime that has been filled with many challenges, one that has seen me experience many similar emotional experiences to the women who come to the clinics and camps. I feel I can relate to them with empathy and compassion and not with criticism or judgement.

I have always had an interest in being able to help yourself. When I eventually decided to change my life and sort things out, Oprah became high on my viewing list and Dr Phil was on my reading list! After years of working on myself and trying to understand what had gone before and what could be ahead, I discovered that the choices I had made as a thirteen-year-old child, a teenage wife, a mother and a daughter were not wrong, they were part of a series of events that led me to where I am today. I look at these choices quite differently now. As it turned out I didn't do such a bad job anyway!

Not so long ago I took myself down to one of our local beaches to have a long think. The mature, grounded woman I am now sat on the beach and had a conversation with the frightened, isolated teenage mother I had been. I told that child mum that it was okay and that she had done a good job – she did the best she could with what she had. She had successfully raised a beautiful, well-rounded, responsible daughter. She was a good mother and she no longer needed to lie about her age or that of her child for fear of what people might think. I told her to be at peace with herself, to no longer be fearful of the criticism and the gossip. I left that teenage mother on the beach that day, and as I walked away I realised she has been one of my greatest strengths, one of my greatest teachers and I am so pleased I finally made the time to get to know her.

Most of the research I did over the years I did for myself and myself alone. David motivated me to change; the example he gave me, of living life the way he does, was inspiring and I wanted to be more like him. Of course, it takes many, many years to 'undo' many, many years so I am a work in progress and a long way off being finished! I have come to believe that we truly need to look deep within ourselves and face the reality of where we are at, who we are and what we have or do not have for us to embrace our life and get the most we can out of it.

I am at a point in my life now where I can take the time to pause and reflect upon many things – is this what they call wisdom? Who knows! I do, however, ask myself 'Why was I picked for this particular journey? What is it all about? What is this hunger to get the message out to women to not feel isolated and alone so that they can empower themselves to lead bigger, better lives?' To be honest I don't really understand what it is all about, and the moment I feel as if I might be getting closer to the answer it floats away again! I do, however, believe in 'it'.

It is not hard to see a correlation between this and my early years. I felt I was never good enough. People can be very quick to put labels on others at best, or at worst to ignore altogether people they feel a little uncomfortable with, as if they don't exist. Maybe if they ignore them they will go away? I don't want anyone to feel the way I did. I want to help as many women as I possibly can. I feel that I am here as a conduit for something that is part of a greater purpose in the work I do. It seems to me that I was hand-picked for this life's mission out of all the women in the world. I don't know anyone else in the world who does what I do; it feels as if there is some higher purpose or force at work. It is the spiritual side of me trying to help people.

I have come to accept that my spirituality is the most powerful side of me. I believe it was this that always reminded me, 'You are worth more than this, Sandi. Don't accept how you are being treated. Go out and find something better for yourself in the world.' Sounds a little weird doesn't it? There was a voice somewhere encouraging me, and knowing that gave me the courage to keep moving on. I didn't understand (and actually still don't) the where, what or why – it was just something I knew and always did and always have. I don't ever remember not having it there.

If there is something bigger and greater out there, it is directing me to do what I do. It enables me to bring everything together – heart, body and soul. I need to continually be open to this. I think we all do. Everyone has a spiritual side no matter how deeply buried it may be. If we are unable to recognise that, we will struggle to find our true meaning and authenticity. It is not about external greatness afforded to us by others, it is about what motivates you, what moves and shakes you and brings you a sense of peace and satisfaction. If you find the authenticity of who you are then you will find peace – it is using your intuition at its highest level.

When I am training with women, something will pop out of my mouth from time to time and they'll turn to me wide-eyed and say, 'Where did that come from?' It has obviously hit a chord with them, hit the nail on the head with whatever it is they are doing or feeling. I can't really say where it came from – it just was there.

If you follow a religion, whether you are an actively practising churchgoer or just live your life by your beliefs you will understand the meaning of spirituality. I admire the qualities of the Christian faith. They are a wonderful set of principles and guidelines to live your life by.

Women know there is something bigger at work. It is in their DNA. It is part of being a woman. Call it intuition, call it spirituality, it doesn't really matter what label you put on it, women know it, live it and feel it. If they become disconnected with themselves for whatever reason, more often than not other women will help them reconnect and rediscover themselves and it is a joy to watch. The power that can be created amongst women to help one another never ceases to amaze me. I find it inspiring to be part of this amazing phenomenon. No matter how dark a place a woman may find herself in, more often than not she will dig deep into her very being and find the strength to lift herself up. It is a joy and a thrill to be there and help her up if and when she needs a helping hand.

Women have traditionally given more of themselves than they take – it comes with the territory of being the nurturers of the human race. I feel that many women I have seen at the clinics and camps end up in the state they are in through a lack of love and understanding from the people who are meant to love them the most – their family. They are raw and emotionally vulnerable.

Lack of confidence in riding has a stigma attached to it. To some, admitting you have lost your confidence means that you are also admitting to being inadequate and/or incompetent. Nothing could be further from the truth though. It takes real strength of character to put aside the bluff and bravado, to expose your vulnerabilities and admit that you need help.

The outpouring of raw emotion that I see time and time again from the women who come for help is because, finally, they know they are understood by someone who has walked the same path and truly feels their pain. I am only just a little further down the road than they are because I started earlier but I am still on that same journey with them. The other women who have come to the clinics are at a similar stage of their journey. They are able to allow other women, total strangers, to see their inner soul without fear of rejection or judgement. I do not see myself as the creator of this metamorphosis – I am the facilitator, allowing the women to come together as one.

In the security and intimacy of the group many secrets reveal themselves. I have seen women finally feel comfortable enough to let go of long hidden and dark secrets of which they have felt deeply ashamed and which they have been carrying guiltily for years. I am talking about sexual abuse. Some of them were victims as children, some as teenagers, some as adults – some have never been free of this abuse. It is heartbreaking to hear their stories but I am also filled with a sense of enlightenment and hope as they make the first steps on the road to reclaiming their autonomy and self-worth. I encourage them and steer them in the right direction to seek professional help. I make sure I follow up with them afterwards if they want to keep the communication open with me. It is such an honour and a privilege to be able to help these wonderful, brave women.

Some women are brought to their knees with emotion and a sense of utter despair lingers within them. It is when they realise they can finally let go that gut-wrenching sobs emanate from deep within their souls. It is as if they are weeping for all the injustices inflicted upon the women of the world throughout time. It is a deeply moving, personal and spiritual experience for all who are privy to the awakening of a new chapter in a woman's life. There is real hope and power in the room during these and so many other moments. Through the nurturing support that women find they also start to gain the strength they need to reinvent themselves – no matter how dark their past has been. Isn't it odd that this all happens because women so want to find that emotional and spiritual connection with their horses and so are brought together? Actually, I said earlier that I saw myself as the facilitator in all of this but perhaps I have a co-facilitator and that is the mystical and spiritual power of the horse.

Some women are very loud when expressing their frustrations and emotions. It is plain to see their suffering. Others are quiet and withdrawn, while still others are bitter and angry and have such a negative, toxic vibe it is a challenge to all around them to be in their presence. Nearly everybody is able to find the help they need to resolve their issues. It may only take a little kindness and patience coupled with a bit of time to make it all turn around. Very occasionally (thank goodness) I come across someone who just cannot be helped. They are unwilling to change, unwilling to see they may need to adjust some of their behaviours or attitudes. I have often tried to redirect them in their thoughts but to no avail. When this occurs I just have to face up to the fact that at that particular moment I cannot help, so I leave them alone for a while. I do not see this as a failure on my part, it is just something that can't be forced. To me, failure is when you don't even try to do something. When you run with an idea and it doesn't work, you haven't failed – you have had a go! I do not see failure as trying new things – it can be as simple as doing the right thing at the wrong time, so how can that be called a failure? You haven't failed if you haven't quit.

Chapter 20

Women who have inspired me

I am continually inspired by the many women I am privileged to meet because of what I do. We can all learn from one another and you never really know where you will get information from. Sometimes it is from the most unlikely places. I believe that in order to lead the best possible life you can, to live your 'authentic life' you have to be open-minded and flexible, be a good listener, have a large ability to feel and listen to others' stories with empathy and, above all, be adaptable and compassionate.

We all have role models whose inspiration we tap into from time to time. You know what I mean, those people we think about when we need a little push along or are struggling or maybe are a little stagnant and directionless. There are several women in my life who have stood out for me and I have used their unique qualities as a source of inspiration in my endeavours to grow as a woman and a human being.

As luck would have it, due to my work I have come across two women in the last few years whose paths would not normally cross mine. From their love of horses and their confidence issues they found their way to my door and I am very grateful for that. They are from very different backgrounds to me but are similar to one another. There are two main differences between the two women. First, one is a very experienced horsewoman, having owned and ridden horses most of her life, while the other took up riding in her early forties. Second, one is married with her four young adult children living at home; the other is divorced, a career woman and with children who are married and parents themselves. They inspire me because they are both strong, independent, educated, highly intelligent women with their feet planted firmly on the ground. They are logical thinkers and are the most emotionally and spiritually healthy women I know. They both have an inward strength and an outward beauty that I love. I really enjoy spending time with them and when I do I realise they have led their lives with integrity, honesty and respect for others – something I know I was not all that flash at doing for many years.

These two ladies are trailblazers for womankind; they are gracious and dignified, and wonderful students. They are highly competent in their personal and professional lives and conduct themselves with dignity and respect, but when they come into the arena they are not afraid to show their vulnerability and fear. That to me is a truly complete person – someone who knows who they are, where they fit in and has it all figured out! It is nice to see that they know it is not a sign of weakness or incompetence to show their fear because they can allow themselves to be nurtured and taught to overcome it. It is inspiring to see such competent women be so emotional and in touch with their feelings in a healthy, upfront manner. They do not overthink the situation, they do not overanalyse it and brood over it, they just accept it for what it is and get on with learning how to overcome it through knowledge, hard work and education.

Both women have had traumas and triumphs in their lives, but they do not let the negatives dictate how they should conduct their lives. They remain true to themselves and you always know where you stand with them. Their response to any situation is an experienced and educated response, not a hysterical and irrational one. They are both dear friends and we consider them part of our family and love them for who they are and how they enrich our lives. They are my true friends through thick and thin – our relationships have developed way beyond that of coach and student. I consider it a privilege to have two such wonderful women in my life. Needless to say, even though they didn't know one another beforehand they get on pretty well together now.

There are other women whose stories have also touched and inspired me. One of these women sadly is no longer with us. She came to one of my clinics many years ago. She was like many of the women I have worked with – extremely emotionally challenging and challenged. Women such as this carry with them such anger and are very much victims in their own life. In fact, it is as if they do not want to be anything other than that – angry victims. They can be quite a challenge to the dynamics of the group. Just as in any gathering of people, one person can ruin the dynamics and harmony of the group. In the clinics and camps someone such as this will shut down any warmth and love that may be within the group as the other participants withdraw emotionally and become guarded in the sea of negativity and self-destruction bellowing from the perpetrator. When this presents itself I understand that I have to keep a filter on what is going on. In my experience these super-angry, super-cynical victims just need to be heard but they often only want to listen to their own repetitive rhetoric and not to what anyone else in the group may have to contribute. I will often take women like this aside at various times and work with them on their own. I give them the time to let it all come bubbling out – I listen – and I let them know they are being heard.

Let's call this super-angry woman whose story I would like to recall, Tracey. Tracey was suffering terminal cancer. Like so many other women I have met with a terminal illness, she knew that she had lost her permission to waste any more of her time but boy was she mad! I learnt that she had been mad and angry with the world before she was diagnosed with cancer. She was hard, opinionated, contrary and offended more people than I care to think about. She started training with both David and I out of desperation with her horse. It became her sole focus in what little time she had left. She was so determined to ride and train that she would come straight from her many chemo sessions to us, shunts and drains still in place. Her hair dropped out, she became sicker and sicker but still she came. As the cancer spread throughout her body she lost the use of her left arm so we adapted the training program to accommodate this.

Tracey trained with us for two or three years with her horse, whom she adored. He was her reason to keep fighting, to keep trying. He was an old horse and one day life, with all of its mysteries that perhaps only make sense at a higher level, took this horse from her. He had to be put down – his journey with her was over. She rang me that day and said, 'I can go now too, Sandi.' She died two weeks later. She gave herself permission to be at peace and to let go.

It was during the course of writing this book that I met another woman with a terminal illness, Robyn. I had the privilege of meeting her only very briefly at one of my clinics. She has affected me in such a powerful way it is hard to put it into words. Meeting her and what transpired is undoubtedly the most profound and important moment in my career so far.

It was at the end of a long, hot summer in Victoria. In fact it wasn't even summer – we were almost to the middle of autumn but Melbourne was going for a record-breaking ten days in a row over 30 °C. The clinic was being held in a rural community some 80 kilometres outside of Melbourne. I travelled up there regularly and it was where my first clinic had been held just after Equitana in 2003. I was looking forward to catching up with some familiar faces.

I knew in advance there were some women coming who didn't have horses so I loaded up the ever reliable and patient Beau (David's multi-talented, long-suffering doll of a horse) and Pistol, who was a new addition to the herd – a gorgeous chestnut and white paint gelding who was as sweet and calm as he was striking. One of my dearest friends, Vicki, had also agreed to bring her mare, Ellie, so that someone could enjoy the clinic with her. I had found Ellie for Vicki several years ago and she was a godsend as Vicki had only started to ride in her forties and had a bad hip so needed a patient, super quiet horse. Ellie was exactly that, a small chestnut quarter horse mare who had been a very successful reiner in her day so was well travelled and educated, though she preferred the life she led now with Vicki, being fussed over and loved and tootling along quietly and calmly without too much pressure. They were a perfect match!

All in all there were twelve women riding at the clinic and a handful of 'fence-sitters' or observers. At the end of the day one of the fence-sitters came to me and said, 'I'm wondering if I can ask you a favour?'

'Sure,' I said.

'I don't know why but I have this overwhelming feeling that I need to come back tomorrow with a friend of mine,' she explained. 'I was only coming today but I would really like to come back tomorrow and bring her with me. But before you say yes I think there is something I should tell you …' I thought this was odd – what was it about her friend that she needed to tell me?

She proceeded to explain that her friend, Robyn, had a terminal brain tumour. She had had operation after operation and there was no more that could be done for her. She had only just got out of hospital after her last operation and was told to go home as no more could be done. She wasn't expected to live for more than another couple of weeks.

The next day all the other women and I were sitting in the circle having a chat and about twenty minutes later, Robyn and her friend arrived. There was no mistaking how gravely ill she was. I watched her come into the shed. Slowly and painfully she walked towards us, a scarf covering her head but peeping out beneath it was an angry, defiant gash, a remnant from her last operation. She was as frail and fragile as a tiny bird, heartache, pain and suffering etched into her eyes which were dull and sunken in her face. Her skin was grey and there was not an ounce of flesh on her bones.

As Robyn eased herself slowly into a chair beside me I could not help myself and I reached down and took her tiny fleshless hand in mine. Her vulnerability and fragility were palpable. I was filled with such compassion and sadness for her. The love and compassion the other women felt was also evident. Robyn didn't join in the conversation but listened quietly and intently as everyone discussed what they had learnt the day before and shared a little of themselves with one another.

When it was time to go out and start work with the horses, Robyn was helped by her friend to a nice shady spot and a comfortable chair by the arena so they could sit and watch. The tenderness with which she attended to Robyn was endearing – it was very clear that they were very good friends and were at ease in one another's company. I wondered what she was thinking and how Robyn's terminal illness and looming departure from this world was affecting her. No doubt she was thinking about how this may well be one of the last times they would spend together, just sitting quietly and watching – being at peace with one another and the day as it unfolded. No drugs, no hospital – just two friends sharing a day with one another.

A thought popped into my mind which I put on hold for most of the day until the opportunity presented itself to act upon it. The woman who had been riding Ellie was getting tired and sore and decided to end her day a little earlier than the others. Vicki, Ellie's owner, was down the other end of the arena helping one of the women so I took Ellie once her rider had dismounted. 'Robyn, would you like to come into the arena and pat Ellie?' I asked. With help she got up and came over to the fence and said yes. I then added, 'I think you should take your thongs off and put your boots on before you come in – it's not a good idea to wear thongs around a horse.'

She came into the arena with her boots on. She was so tired she was barely audible when she spoke, her voice tiny and distant even though she was right beside me. She reached out and patted Ellie gently on the neck. Ellie stood rock still, her eyes soft and gentle as Robyn stroked her neck then her face. Robyn put her cheek against Ellie's nose on the side where a horse's nose is soft and velvety and warm. Ellie closed her eyes a little with pleasure. We all stood there quietly for ten minutes or so while Robyn gently explored Ellie's face, her ears and her neck with her hands.

Robyn turned to me and said, 'Everyone tells me I used to have horses in my life and that I was a quite good rider. I don't know, I have no memory of this. Since my surgery I can't remember – I can't remember anything – I have no memories … ' Her voice trailed off as she seemed to be lost in thought, struggling to dig up some vague recollections of something, anything, from her past.

I can't imagine what it would be like to have no memories – it is our memories and our experiences that mould us, define us, give us a sense of who we are, where we have been and where we belong. I was stunned by the thought that someone was standing in front of me with no memory of anything – no wonder there was a sense of bewilderment and fright in her eyes.

'That's okay,' I said. 'How would you feel about getting on?'

'No,' she said slightly panicky. 'I couldn't! I am too scared!'

'What are you scared of?' I asked her.

'I'm scared of falling off!'

'Robyn, you need to trust me,' I said. 'You need to believe in yourself and believe in me. I believe in you and I know this horse is as safe as safe can be and my training system is as safe as houses. Believe in yourself Robyn; I shall be right here beside you, nothing will happen, you won't fall off. I promise.'

She looked at me and said, 'Okay, I trust you. I believe you.'

I led Ellie over to the mounting block, which was a great big old tractor tyre – wide and solid. Ellie did as she had been trained to do and stood there with the patience of an angel as Robyn leaned into me and almost became my second skin. I put my foot into the stirrup behind her leg and foot and enveloped her body in my arms – I half mounted Ellie and then just as Robyn was halfway up I backed down and with her friend's help we popped her into the saddle. Ellie didn't move a muscle, didn't twitch an ear. It was as if she knew her responsibility and she did it admirably. Robyn sat there for ten minutes rubbing Ellie's wither and her shoulder, running her fingers through her mane; not a word was spoken.

A hush and a stillness came over the clinic – all the other women were watching from the far end of the arena. Every single one of us could feel the emotion welling up inside Robyn as she sat there silently, gently rubbing Ellie's neck, ensconced in the warmth of the life underneath the horse's burnished chestnut coat. Robyn's tears splashed down onto Ellie's coat, making dark rivulets along her sides. I can only hazard a guess as to what those tears meant – I think they were tears of gratitude, tears for memories long lost, tears for the life she may have yet lived if the crippling insidious tumour had never inveigled itself into her brain. But most of all I think they were tears of love and acceptance and for the peace she had found in that moment.

'Are you ready for a walk?' I asked. Robyn nodded and as Ellie slowly and delicately picked her way forward past the mounting block and around the arena, the whole clinic cheered and applauded. They knew what they were seeing – they knew what a special moment they were all witness to.

I walked with Robyn and Ellie for a while and then I called Robyn's friend over and together they walked around and around the arena for fifteen or twenty minutes. Most of the time they were silent but every now and then they would share a joke or a conversation. They were like two schoolgirls out walking and riding and sharing the one pony as they enjoyed the long summer school holidays together. They looked happy and safe in one another's company. The horse quietly walked with her ears flickering backwards and forwards as if she too was listening in to odd pieces of the conversation.

'I'm ready to get off now,' Robyn finally said and so I stood up on the mounting block and mirror-imaged her back down again. Robyn turned and hugged me when she got off. 'I remember, I remember now,' she said. 'I used to ride horses. Thank you Sandi for giving me back that memory.' She turned back to face Ellie and put her arms around her neck and buried her head in her mane. I heard her whisper softly to Ellie, 'Thank you Ellie, you have given me the greatest gift you can, thank you.'

As Robyn turned back to me I saw something different in her eyes. There was a tiny flickering light, a warmth, a sense of contentment and peace. 'Whenever you are at your darkest moment or hour over the next little while, Robyn,' I said to her, 'remember this moment, remember the strength and courage you found within yourself and the fact that you believed in yourself. Hold onto this memory.'

'When I get to heaven, Sandi, I am going to ask God to send down more people like you!' Robyn replied. 'Thank you Sandi, you have given me something very special indeed – this is the happiest I can ever remember being. God bless you.'

I gave everything I could to Robyn that day – all of my emotional and spiritual energy. There was nothing left for me to give but it was one of the best moments of my life. I packed up and left the clinic feeling totally drained but in a very positive way. I know I shall never see Robyn again and at the moment I do not know why it was that she crossed my path but I am filled with gratitude that I was there to share those moments with her. It is a memory I shall carry with me forever. I feel not only did I help her but it is as if she gave me a gift as well, though I wasn't sure what it was at the time.

Robyn had the purest of hearts and what I do know is that for me she makes life, in all of its wondrous, tumultuous, sometimes challenging and daunting glory, very real. She epitomises all there is in the messages of life in the biggest and brightest way possible – she was everything all wrapped up into one fragile package with the heart and courage of a lion.

I went home at the end of that weekend and felt absolutely exhausted and drained for a couple of days. It wasn't too long before I was on a plane to Perth for another clinic. And then during the course of the weekend it came to me – I had a light bulb moment, which I love – about what it was that Robyn had given to me. I realised that, even though she was facing a certain and imminent death, Robyn had not given up on seeing the beauty of life in every moment. There was clarity to her understanding of life and I realised that I saw before me a much stronger, more defined woman than I was. It took me a couple of days to figure this out and I understood that what Robyn had taught me was that I had so much more growing to do – that my journey was nowhere near complete either personally or spiritually, and I became really excited and very grateful.

I live a very busy lifestyle and travel a lot. I need to work really hard at being still – still within myself, finding my inner sense of peace. When things present themselves to me I work through them so that I can be better at what I do. I have created a lot of peace within my life in comparison to how I used to live and how I used to feel but it is nowhere near enough. This is my new project, my new focus and I know there will only be very positive rewards for me, my family, my friends and the women I help in my clinics and camps. Thank you, Robyn, for sharing this gift with me.

Not all of the women I meet have sad stories. Many of them are absolute characters like Betty.

It was a really hot weekend, one of the last absolute scorchers of the summer in southern Australia, when Betty came to a clinic. I watched the ladies tootle into the cool of the dairy for the clinic, which had been organised for some months at a new location. The coordinator had chairs set up, the kettle was on and everyone made themselves a cuppa. The participants had already unloaded their horses and put them in the yards. I started the clinic with the circle, asking them a little about themselves and why they were there.

I saw her walk in quietly. She looked a little shy and uttered an apology for being late. She came with a friend as a fence-sitter to see what it was all about. I noticed she walked with that slight sway people have when they have pain or discomfort in their hips. She was not young – I learnt later that she was sixty-seven. Her kind, weathered face was crinkled and battered from years of being a worker and living an outdoor life – I knew that look well. It is the sort of face you see throughout the Australian bush on the men and women of this vast and sometimes harsh land we live in; their faces are weathered by years in the sun and the rain, their smiles and sorrows etched in deep lines on their skin for all to see.

When it came time for Betty to tell her story she leant forward slightly with her hands clasped in her lap; it was as if she was going to tell the group a secret for our ears only. She had several horses that she had owned for years – I don't recall there being one younger than twenty years old amongst them all! She hadn't ridden for years and yet I could see her eyes light up and her soul brighten momentarily when she thought about riding. Then her face would cloud over again and she would lean back slightly as a lethargy overcame her – 'Of course I am not very fit any more … if I could get fit again perhaps I could ride again …' A spark of hope would cross her face.

As her thoughts meandered to younger days, fitter days, days where she was physically less vulnerable in the saddle, she would lean forward again and it was so engaging, so entrancing. And then just as suddenly her thoughts were clouded by her doubt, by her lack of self-belief. I felt that the time was right for her to be here – I was excited by the possibilities of what may unfold for her that weekend.

I am not sure how she came to tell us a most remarkable story about one of her horses. He was twenty-five now and he owed his life to her. He was an ex-galloper and apparently showed quite a turn of speed and quite a bit of talent. Unfortunately he, like so many gallopers, had been subjected to some of the most barbaric training methods used by less scrupulous trainers, which you hear of from time to time in the racing industry. He began to baulk in the barriers and would not jump out of them cleanly after a couple of starts. Solution? Put cattle prods on him to zap him out of the barriers. It may work for a while but a horse's brain is fried and their adrenaline and anxiety levels escalate to monumental proportions, making them a danger to themselves and all those around.

Betty knew of this horse and ended up taking him home and working with him. Not surprisingly she took her time and was able to help this poor, tortured soul regain his confidence and had him walking in and out of the barriers again without any fear. The horse's trainer and owner wanted to put him back on the track to continue to build on his previous racing success, so he and Betty came to an agreement: once he had finished racing Betty would be given the horse. She could keep him and call him her horse. They shook on it, as she said to us, 'We had a gentleman's agreement – or so I thought.'

The horse's racing career saw him go to Darwin and Betty eventually lost track of him. However, as fate would have it she made enquiries about him from time to time and discovered he had ended his career and was on a station in the Territory being used as a stockhorse. A friend helped her track him down and she organised to have him sent back to her home in Victoria.

Somehow or other his old owner heard of his return and Betty tells the story of how she wasn't home at the time but she got a call from her husband, telling her that the bloke had rung and was on his way over to pick up the horse – to take him back! Betty flew home and found her husband's pistol (a Derringer). She waited for the ex-owner and when he appeared to take what was now her horse after their 'gentleman's agreement' she pointed the gun at his head (unloaded, she told us, as she didn't know how to load it – not that she would if she did!) and told him she would kill him if he ever came near her or her horse again!

I looked at the other women as this story unfolded – some were shocked, some laughed, some cheered 'Good for you!' It was quite a yarn! Betty went to court over this incident, the judge scolding her for her actions and putting her on a twelve-month good behaviour bond, and amusedly she told us she couldn't ever hold a firearm licence. But the judge did agree that the handshake, the gentleman's agreement, meant that this lucky horse was indeed hers in the eyes of the law and put the matter to rest.

Betty's eyes shone with love and gratitude as she told the story – they twinkled with mischief from time to time as she recalled the details. Her love and commitment to this horse and her sense of fair play was inspiring. I was so pleased she had shared her story with the group. Her calm, grandmotherly presence was a gift to all of us there on that hot summer morning. Betty's presence whispered to me of a bygone era, where people cherished and respected their horses and their dogs, their loyalty to their family and friends was paramount to their moral fibre and our country was moulded underneath the toil of their labours – thoroughly decent, hard-working men and women.

I was so pleased Betty had come to spend time with us that weekend.
I was even more delighted when the next day she arrived with a float
and one of her horses – a chestnut mare who had not been off her
property for years and had not been ridden for over a year or so. Out in
the scorching sun she absorbed every bit of information she could and
then practised what she'd learnt. Her reflexes and coordination were a
little slow and rusty at first – her manoeuverability was not quite as
sprightly as some of the other participants but her focus and
commitment was unfailing. By the end of the day she was on her horse!
Up and down she got, up and down. Her darling horse stood rock still
as Betty clambered ever so slowly and awkwardly aboard. It was as if the
mare knew she had to stay still to look after this special soul. Betty's
determination and the inspiration she felt meant she did not feel the
pain in her hips as she was mounting. The look on her face was priceless.
A broad grin spread from ear to ear – she sat up there gently patting her
horse and saying thank you to her. When she got off a lone tear trickled
down her face. She was so moved by what she had achieved – she said it
was one of the best days she could remember in such a long time.

I am so very fortunate to be living the life I am. It is a gift and a
blessing to meet beautiful women like Betty; they enrich my life more
than they can ever know and I am so inspired by each and every one of
them. Their love, their compassion, their humility inspires me and fills
me with gratitude. They also have that effect on the other women at the
clinics and camps, I am sure. For some who feel they are getting a little
old, meeting someone like Betty in her late sixties, physically restricted

in her movement but still getting on her horse, is inspirational enough; for others, hearing her story and being enveloped in her calm, gentle nature is soothing and comforting. Still others may just relish the sheer joy of hearing a like-minded soul with a deep love and passion for the common bond all the horsey ladies of the world share. Thank goodness for the Betty's of this world!

Chapter 21

In their own words

People are always intrigued by the interaction of horses and humans, and the connection of women and horses is even more compelling. There is an undeniable attraction to horses that many little girls experience and the connection that a woman can develop with a horse is quite different than that of a man. Generally speaking, men see the horse similar to a piece of machinery or a work tool, there is little emotional attachment to the horse. For women the involvement and connection with a horse can be a deeply emotional experience. It is hard to identify whether it is spiritual or a basic instinct from times long gone but it is undeniable. Riding or even handling a horse is something many people have anxiety about, yet the achievement of it is empowering, uplifting and potentially life changing.

Sandi tells her story to many of her clinic participants, including how she took steps to regain her confidence with riding; to me there is still a vulnerability there that she so willingly shares. That takes guts – guts to tell everyone how low she was and guts to expose her vulnerability. She uses her story as a gift to all and does it selflessly – it is free to anyone who wants it. The gift of enabling women to see what is possible through understanding ourselves, by others understanding that we all have 'stuff' to deal with and tackling the hard issues (before we even get on our horses!). Sandi sees it as her obligation to 'help' other women but she does so much more than that – she adopts many of them (including myself) as what I know will be lifelong friends. So much of what Sandi does is only partly related to the horses – they are sometimes just the means of connection. Almost everyone who attends one of Sandi's camps has a teary moment or two and many women have an epiphany – no exaggeration. At Equitana demonstrations, I have witnessed women in tears as Sandi connects to their souls, fears or hopes – I was one of those in 2005.

Sandi is selfless with what she has to offer, tough on what she expects based on her already working out what you are capable of, is welcoming to all, has compassion to rival Mother Theresa towards those in need but does not suffer fools gladly, has the energy of a hundred women when on a mission, has the gift of the gab, the propensity for fun of a fifteen-year-old and a heart of gold that could be mined!

Vicki

I have loved horses from when I was a little girl. Back then I was a 'paddock basher' like a lot of kids — just get on and ride. There wasn't much finesse about it, I just wanted to be around horses. I hung out at the local riding school helping wherever I could. I never actually owned my own horse but shared one with my sister in my early teens. She was a failed riding school horse!

Then I grew up and horses went out of my life until my mid thirties. I ended up having a pretty high-profile, high-pressure career which sent me overseas and further and further away from horses. But they were never far from my mind, and while my career saw me develop some characteristics that enabled my 'survival' within the profession they were not really who I truly was. In my mid thirties I had a life change and was able to return to Australia and seek out a more conducive rural lifestyle. I bought my first horse, sight unseen — yikes! The alarm bells should have gone off. The first horse I had ever owned just by myself was an unrideable Arab! He was then replaced by what was meant to be a 'confidence builder'. He managed to break three of my ribs and shatter what little confidence I had. Not to be deterred and being who I am I also bought an unbroken two-year-old amongst all of this so that I could start riding him when I had got my mojo back again on the older ones! Hmm … the two-year-old went off to be broken in and became my number one horse. I was a showie and it was my dream to show this baby myself — that's what I really wanted to do but I pretty soon realised that emotionally I was way out of my depth.

There had to be a solution. I searched and searched and over and over the name 'Sandi Simons' kept popping up. So in October 2008 I hooked my float up and drove nine hours to one of Sandi's Confidence Camps. I was sick with anxiety and doubt. When I arrived at the first camp I was an angry, broken woman who thought that if Sandi's camp didn't work for me my dreams with horses would be over. I had poured so much time, money and energy into horses that it was taking an enormous emotional toll on me and if I couldn't come back with any answers then it was all over as far as I was concerned.

It was one of the best things I have ever done for myself. I drove home at the end of the week feeling light-hearted and alive and I had a bag full of tools I could use to help me with my horses. I went to three more of Sandi's camps and have nearly finished my training course with her husband David. I have nothing but praise, admiration and respect for Sandi as she helped me turn my life around and fulfil my childhood dream!

Carol

A friend of mine was going to one of David's clinics in 2002 in Tatura and wondered if I wanted to come. So I packed up the two feral horses I owned at the time and went. It was fantastic – I was awestruck! Sandi was there too, tootling around in the background and although she had her horse, Galli, there she was really there supporting David and helping organise things.

She did the paperwork, took the money, met everyone and got everyone organised.

It was obvious to me that she was the 'power behind the throne' and it was because of her support and good business brain that David could concentrate on what he did best – training. They were complementary to one another – a good mix.

I was so impressed with David and his training methods that after a while I decided to do the trainers course with him. It was during this time that I got to know Sandi better. I soon learnt that she was a totally natural, spontaneous, dynamic woman and what you saw is what you got. There was nothing at all contrived or superficial about her. Initially, a couple of times, I was a little taken aback by her unabashed upfront manner when I was staying with them in their home – she said what she thought, she had high standards for all of those around her and everyone, no matter who you were, was expected to pull their weight. Her direct approach to all of those around her was just something I was not used to and at times I found myself floundering a bit and not sure where to put myself.

I soon came to realise that she was an amazing woman who day in day out tried really hard to learn about herself, the people around her and what made her and them tick. She was continually striving to improve herself and her life and was a warm and sympathetic woman with a heart of gold.

By the end of 2005 I had nearly finished my trainers course with David, and Sandi had been running her Confidence Clinics for over a year. The next one was scheduled to be at Tyabb on my side of the bay. She asked me to come and assist. After the clinic she came to me and said, 'I've got a business proposition for you.' And that is when my friendship and professional relationship with her really started to bloom.

I went with Sandi to all of her Confidence Clinics as her assistant. They were very popular with women of all ages that a second pair of eyes and hands was needed so that everyone got the maximum benefit from being there. I have been to every live-in camp since the first one in May 2006.

Through it all I have seen Sandi grow and develop as she has learnt from the women who have come and shared their life stories with her and the other women at the camp. Sandi has the most unique ability to tap into what it is that is holding these women back from achieving their dreams and goals in the saddle and ultimately in their lives. We have been witness to some really sad, awful stories around the circle, which commences with a cuppa every morning at every clinic and camp. We have laughed until our sides have hurt, shed many tears and seen lots of light bulbs go off! It has been a wonderful journey that we have shared and do share together, and it is a privilege to work with her as she offers something unique to all of the women around the world who love horses and want to ride.

Sandi is passionate about people leading the best life that they can and she continually challenges herself and those around her to do the same. She is always reading, researching, talking to people to gather as much knowledge as she can to help the women who come to her with confidence issues. She is an inspiration to us all and I am proud to be associated with her both personally and professionally.

Sandi didn't like how my former husband treated me. She questioned me often about the relationship and was never shy about voicing her thoughts. I always replied, 'Oh, but I love him'. I now hear that echo in my clients towards their unruly horses. She also didn't like the horse I had at the time as the mare was opinionated and I had fallen off her numerous times. Sandi used to say, 'I am not going to come visit you in hospital!' I really didn't start to understand what she was on about until after Black Saturday took all my inanimate possessions. I started to realise that life is urgent. Later that year she organised a surprise fortieth for me. The thing that had the biggest impact was something she wrote on a teddy that she had everyone sign. Sandi wrote, 'My darling friend, I will always have your back, no matter where or when!! I love you more than words can express. Your sleeping partner, Sandi xx.'

The penny dropped. I realised none of that was true of my former husband ... Sandi was a pillar of support following the fires, my separation and divorce.

Another moment when I became clear on who Sandi is as a woman was one of her birthdays. As usual there was a gaggle of women at her house. We all sat around her dinner table, consuming our beverage of choice. Sandi instigated a conversation, having us declare who we were for each other. 'I said to the group that I admired how Sandi often took it upon herself to encourage the women she meets to realise that it is important and totally acceptable for them to believe in themselves and stand up for what is right for them.

The next morning, Dave said, 'I understand all the empty bottles left around, but what's with the tissues?' He's such a bloke!

Annie

I was a 'late starter' with horses. I had always wanted to own a horse since I was a little girl but we lived in the city, which made that impossible. When my husband and I were first married we moved around a lot as he was in the navy, so that was not conducive to owning a horse.

Our daughter had a pony as a child so this was the first horse I had had any ongoing contact with. Eventually we settled in one spot and at the age of forty-eight I bought my first horse. I still have him. He is the perfect first horse – quiet, chilled out and a little dull. I have never had any fear of him as he has never done anything to make me feel frightened.

I was thirsty for knowledge and wanted to learn as much as I could as quickly as possible about all aspects of horsemanship. I eventually found my way to Sandi – her name would pop up from time to time amongst other horsey people and so one day I picked up the phone to book into one of her Confidence Camps. That was in October 2009.

Unlike many of the other women at the camp I didn't have a confidence issue from a fall, a break from riding, an unsuitable horse or any of the other reasons that presented themselves. I just wanted to learn more and do more. I was looking for, I thought, how to do things with a horse – to attain horse knowledge. It took me a long time to realise that Sandi's camps and clinics were about personal development, using horses as a common denominator. I am from a family and generation who do not inquire into emotions, feelings, moral values, personal values, perceived failings etc., so I have found some of the exercises and questions posed by Sandi extremely confronting and difficult to process. My self-belief and self-confidence are not strong points in my life, horsey and otherwise. I am so impressed with how she can hone in to the essence of a person after listening to them for such a brief time, and she really does hear what you have to say.

In retrospect I now realise that at my first camp the final debrief was the most important time of the whole week. I remember vividly that Sandi listed some of my better character traits and told me I was a 'keeper', meaning that she wanted to see more of me and that we had gone beyond a client/instructor relationship in her mind. I was totally shocked to think that someone like her could think that I had that much to offer! I will never forget that. I still struggle with self-worth but I remember that session and always will. One other thing I value from our interactions, and which is of value in everything I do in life as well as horse training, is Sandi constantly asking what your lesson plan is, which is relevant to every facet of life. I try to always have a lesson plan and use it to improve my attitude to people and horses.

It was a wonderful week being with like-minded women and I was enthralled with the skill and empathy Sandi showed to all of the participants and what major breakthroughs we all made.

Eileen

In May 2011 I had a really bad fall from a horse I had recently bought as a dressage horse. He reared over backwards with me and shattered my elbow and arm as well as totally shattering what confidence I did have as a nearly fifty-year-old rider! I had to have an operation to have the arm pinned and plated and when I was semi-recovered the thought of riding again, even after a lifetime of having ridden and having horses to this day at home, left me more than a little anxious.

Luckily for me I have a wonderfully supportive network of friends and family and far from discouraging me to ride again they were pleased when I found an article in our local paper about Sandi's second clinic in our area. What Sandi was offering seemed to be what I was needing and so I decided to attend. The clinic was only four months after my fall and I had restricted movement in my arm and was in quite a lot of pain as well. I didn't take the offending culprit but instead opted to take to the clinic a mare I had at home. To my very great embarrassment and horror she was absolutely the worst behaved horse there!

The day started with us all getting together with a cuppa and telling the group why we were there. I am a very private person and do not show my emotions easily or publicly but when it came to my turn I couldn't stop crying! All of a sudden all the pent-up emotion I was carrying inside me came bubbling out. The great gift that Sandi gave me that day was that I was allowed to give myself permission to be frightened, to recognise that and to be okay with that rather than trying to battle on, be stoic and cover it all up or push it aside. In addition to this, all of us attending the clinic were given the tools in our approach to our horses to learn how to be safe, take control and have fun with our horses. We learnt how to read the cues the horses were giving us from a different and more aware perspective.

I soon came to realise that I was not being a leader for my horse because of my fear of being hurt again and I did not have the knowledge or tools to remedy the situation. Without direction the horses were at a loss and that was quite literally an accident waiting to happen. I had become a little blasé with my own ability with horses as I had been around them for so long, and now I learnt to become much more safety conscious and be one step ahead of my horse and her emotions – just like any good leader should.

I went back to a second clinic a few months later with the same mare and this time – because I was in a much better headspace and had been using the information and tools that I had learnt from the previous clinic – my mare and I were able to demonstrate to the rest of the group the sacking-out process. Instead of being the worst behaved horse there she was the demonstration horse. What a change!

Sandi's interest in her clients is genuine and does not end when she leaves the clinic – she is always at the end of the phone if you need help with a question, a problem or just some encouragement and redirection. She is a very busy lady but she has the unique ability to always have the time to listen, care and help. I feel very privileged to be able to call her a friend, which indeed she has become; she has seen me at my most vulnerable physically and emotionally. She allowed me to be okay with where I was at.

Since meeting Sandi I have developed as a person away from horses as well. In the same way that I now know how to not be pushed around by my horses but offer them leadership and guidance, I have brought these traits into my day-to-day life. I am able to say 'This is me, take me for who I am and where I am at at the moment'. I won't allow anyone or anything to pressure me into something I don't want to do.

Nearly two years on from my accident I no longer attend clinics but I can't seem to break the habit of being with the Tamworth group who have become such good friends. I have private lessons with Sandi when she comes to Tamworth, which are invaluable to my training of my new horse. I also enjoy helping out when asked in the clinic sessions. I learn so much from watching Sandi and her team and it is wonderful to be able to use the tools learnt on horses other than my own. There is a new confidence in myself when it comes to training my own horses but also in being able to work with others' horses.

At a clinic last October, Sandi suggested I have a lesson with David. I wasn't keen to say the least. I have absolutely nothing against David but found I had an irrational fear of the unknown. I was, however, told by Sandi and another one of their trainers that this was going to happen so I reluctantly went to have my lesson. I can't say I exactly enjoyed it as I was very much out of my comfort zone but at the end of the second lesson I realised that I had really needed the push to take the next step to progress with my riding. It was like standing near the edge of a cliff – I had been happy to stand six feet away from the cliff edge, playing it safe and worrying that I might come to grief if I moved closer. Being made to step forward allowed me to see that the drop was really only six inches and it was perfectly okay. Since that time I have been able to move forward towards goals I set myself – one step at a time!

To show how far I have come, not so very long ago I was at a dressage competition and my usually quiet horse got a fright as an extremely loud motorbike took off right near the arena. He dropped his head and let loose with three bucks. After my initial 'Oh no!' (or something similar!) I took control with an authority I would not have thought possible six months ago and completed the test. He was a little tense at the top end of the arena near where he had been frightened but he was focusing on me. The sense of achievement was fantastic. I had not just survived a situation that gave me flashbacks of my fall but had dealt with it and moved forward. I rang Sandi to share my experience and I can honestly say that I could hear the pride for me in her voice. Yes, there is still apprehension a lot of the time when I ride but I know that I am able to use the training tools. My horses are benefitting from better training and I am starting to get back a part of my life that was shattered along with my arm.

I have gained so much and realise it is perfectly okay to do what you can in life and with your horse – no more, no less. I have given myself permission to take the next step and move forward in a positive and meaningful way. I now realise that what I want out of my horses is safety, enjoyment and the ability to feel that this can be achieved in all areas of life.

Sandi has helped mend me to a very great extent.

Rose

I had ridden as a child and had my own pony. Like most kids I had had the odd tumble or two (or six) off my pony over the years. I remember two bad ones in particular – one when I was in year 2 at school and another when I was in year 7. Unbeknown to me at the time these really knocked me around emotionally and started eating away at my confidence. When I was in my late teens and at uni I started working part-time with a trainer who specialised in cutting horses. I had another really bad fall off one of these horses and broke my back! I didn't get back on a horse for a year and found I was full of fear and anxiety and just could not get on any strange horse. I eventually bought myself an Australian stockhorse and thought that if I owned my own horse and worked on him I would be able to regain my confidence and fulfil my dreams of entering stockhorse classes at comps and maybe even eventually do some camp-drafting.

I found an instructor in my local area and was having regular lessons. We were going along steadily, apart from me constantly apologising to him for everything I did or didn't do! It was nothing to do with him or the lessons, that was just me. Never one to push my own barrow or to feel worthy, I constantly found myself in a state of apology and uncertainty to all those around me.

My mother saw an ad in HorseDeals for a Confidence Clinic with a lady called Sandi Simons, who was coming to our neck of the woods. Mum knew I was struggling a bit and suggested that I might like to go. But first she rang my instructor to ask what he thought. As it turned out he had trained with Sandi and her husband David and thought it would be a great idea for me to go along.

Mum came with me for moral support that weekend and it was one of the most revealing, enlightening, challenging experiences of my life. When we arrived the other participants were all milling around with their horses and as is my way I hung back and stayed in the background so as not to draw attention to myself. The first thing we had to do was sit around a table in a circle as Sandi asked us a bit about ourselves and why we were there – simple enough? Wow! When it came to my turn, Sandi, with her incredible ability and insight, asked me some questions – well, it opened up a floodgate of emotions. I cried and cried and cried. It all came tumbling out – things that even I didn't know I had been hanging onto. From having been a happy, carefree, outgoing, social adolescent and teenager I had gradually become an isolated, cautious, introverted young woman with no confidence and full of self-doubt, always apologising for myself.

My poor mum sat and listened to all of this unfold and she too was crying her eyes out. She knew I had lost some of my confidence with horses but neither she nor I knew how deep-seated it was in all aspects of my life and how debilitating it had become.

When Sandi asked my about the lack of confidence I had and the stress of worrying about what others thought, I can clearly remember her saying, 'The simple stuff you are worrying about is just crap!' This simple sentence has stuck with me since the moment Sandi said it. The stress, heartache and emotions I was caught up in about what people thought of me was, as Sandi said, just crap! This was a light bulb moment for me and has allowed me to learn and practise not sweating the small stuff and to not give time and thought to stuff that is insignificant in my life.

Over the course of the weekend and in the weeks and months that followed Sandi gave me the physical and emotional tools to heal myself, to believe in myself and to allow me to find the person I was before. The 'hangover' I carried with me from my falls into my riding and life in general has dissipated and I now have a soft, responsive, happy horse that I love working with and riding. Before, he was a nice, quiet but rigid and dull horse that just went through the motions – just like me.

I clearly remember the last night of the clinic. I was on my way home and after a huge weekend I was starving. So I stopped at a local restaurant full of people and ordered takeaway – something I could certainly not have done before the clinic. Such a simple thing, ordering dinner, gave me a huge lift and I immediately sent Sandi a message to which I received an ecstatic reply. I also remember the first time I drove a float with horses on board. This was another thing I would not have been able to carry out without the support of Sandi and the amazing clinic.

Sandi has taught me that horses are mirrors of ourselves and that to get anywhere in life, with or without horses, we need to believe. Believe in ourselves, in our horses, in our training. If you believe in yourself then no-one can make you feel worthless. People who say hurtful things about others are filling a void in their own life and are trying to make themselves feel better, and this is something I always have to keep thinking about! Taking with you a sense of gratitude wherever you go is something else that stays with me and something else I have learnt from Sandi. Be grateful for what you have – your friends, your lifestyle, your health, your horses. This very simple concept was something I had lost sight of. I have so much to be grateful for but couldn't see it as I was too wrapped up in my own 'bubble' of stuff. I have now woken up and ventured to look further afield and have seen how incredibly lucky I am!

Sandi said, 'You are a most beautiful young woman and I'm so grateful to have met you and now have you in my life.' This is one of the kindest things someone has ever said to me. It is so hard to write all the beautiful, amazing and kind things Sandi has said to me to make me realise I am worthwhile and deserve to live a happy, fulfilling life, which I aim every day to achieve.

The lesson plans Sandi gave me for my life I will always strive to keep working on. After more than a year from her first clinic I am proud to say that I am a completely different person and I have a transformed horse! We are both happy and loving life, and

I only apologise sometimes! Sandi, my instructor and close friends have always been close by and remind me that I've crossed the line and I'm not going back over it – always look forward!

I can never thank Sandi enough for the gift she has given me. She has given me back my life and I truly treasure each and every day and opportunity that presents itself with my horse and with my life. I am no longer 'going through the motions' as I was before I met Sandi.

Caitlin

Epilogue

I know that I am still evolving and growing as a person and as a woman, just as we all are until the day we take our very last breath. The ongoing journey with the work I do with women, their horses and their confidence issues is far from over. I am excited by the prospect that everyday I am able to continue to teach and conduct clinics and camps to help as many women as possible around the world. I have been asked several times over the years to go and teach in America. I have been to some exhibitions there from time to time but the opportunity to conduct one of my Confidence Clinics had not arisen until recently. In July 2013 I had the privilege to do so with another remarkable group of women in, ironically, a town called Rochester, in Washington. Over the course of the weekend I learnt that the women in the United States are no different than their Australian counterparts and they all hold the same fears, doubts, aspirations and dreams.

When I went to pick up the mail from our letterbox on my return home, my eye caught something flapping around on the ground, splattered with mud. It was a letter from one of the Clinic participants in the US. It touched me deeply that she took the time to write down how she felt and post it to Australia. I felt I wanted to include it in my story as she encapsulates so much of what I hear and see all the time when women feel they do not have a voice and cannot be heard. Fortunately, because of our mystical and beautiful friend, the horse, she was able to find her way to my clinic.

I shall leave you with this and the wish that you too find your voice and follow your dreams and passions no matter where your life may take you ...

'I am starting to be able to find my words to explain what this weekend has meant to me. First off it literally changed my life! I know that sounds cliché but it really did!

I went to your clinic with complete doubt (about myself) that I would learn anything, after all I have spent endless hours with pen and paper standing in front of my TV watching all these 'wonderful' trainers do this and do that and ended up learning nothing!!! I actually ended up feeling more and more inadequate than ever. "Yield this, engage that, lift the shoulder, shoulder over, give here, bend there..." WHAT THE????? I had NO idea what the hell anyone was talking about for crying out loud!!!! This is how I thought it would be at your clinic. I would just nod like I 'get it' so as not to draw attention to myself as the dumb ass in the arena and move on, unnoticed ...

So there we are at your clinic – and there was you!

It was like WE SPOKE THE SAME LANGUAGE AND I KNEW WHAT YOU WERE SAYING – JUST LIKE THAT! Not only did I understand you, I didn't feel like I was an idiot that the teacher had to spend time on whilst looking down upon me with disgust. It was angel-singing awesome!!!

I don't know if you heard me when we were leaving, but I was having a fit because I still couldn't find words to express my feelings for this whole clinic … I couldn't calm down enough to think. We climbed into the truck and I am still babbling on like a weirdo and was telling the girls how words couldn't cover my feelings, about how you affected me and then I just plain said:

I HAVE RIDDEN MY WHOLE LIFE BUT I JUST LEARNED HOW TO RIDE TODAY!!

Thank you Sandi Simons for a great rest of my life! You are locked into my heart forever!

Lori

Love, hugs and happy trails and may your life be worth riding too!

Acknowledgements

Naturally, there are many people who have been an integral part of my life and my story so far and I would like to thank them all for their contribution but especially to David and my children for all their support in writing this book and their resilience for putting up with me!

My parents for encouraging me to have my own voice and loving me unconditionally.

Felicity Wischer who heard what I had to say from our many conversations about my life then went away and put it into the words you have read on these pages. She has spent endless hours that I know about, and many more that I don't, giving my voice its proper expression. I am grateful for her innate ability to be peaceful and present and allowing my words and my story to unfold before us. And now she knows me inside out – warts and all!

All the wonderful horses in my life – if I didn't have them I wouldn't have a life worth riding!

John and Jody Lyons because the greatest thing they have given me is their friendship and the example of how to live life with humility and dignity. They always find the good in everybody and treat people with kindness and respect.

Colleen Lethbridge for throwing me in the deep end at Equitana 2003 and for understanding that I may have an important role in helping women find their authentic selves. She believed in me, and what I had to say, and saw the whole picture even when I didn't know there was one!

To all those wonderful women who have entrusted me with their stories and have attended a clinic or a camp over the years. They have all shared something of themselves with me and enabled me to continue to evolve as a woman, as a trainer, as a friend, a wife and a mother.

Lastly, to all of my beautiful friends I have accumulated on this journey – even though this book is a testament of what you think I give you, it is nowhere near what you actually give to me and for that I thank all of you.

Sandi